An All-Consuming
DESIRE
S*to*CCEED

A Success Formula

John Paul Carinci

NEW YORK

An All-Consuming DESIRE *to* SUCCEED
A Success Formula

by John Paul Carinci
© 2011 John Paul Carinci. All rights reserved.

ISBN 978-1-60037-994-9 (paperback)
Library of Congress Control Number: 2011904735

Published by:
MORGAN JAMES PUBLISHING
The Entrepreneurial Publisher
5 Penn Plaza, 23rd Floor
New York City, New York 10001
(212) 655-5470 Office
(516) 908-4496 Fax
www.MorganJamesPublishing.com

Edited by:
Heidi Mann

Front cover photo provided by
Keta Kosman
www.wildbaldeagles.ca

Cover Design by:
Rachel Lopez
rachel@r2cdesign.com

Interior Design by:
Bonnie Bushman
bbushman@bresnan.net

In an effort to support local communities, raise awareness and funds, Morgan James Publishing donates one percent of all book sales for the life of each book to Habitat for Humanity. Get involved today, visit
www.HelpHabitatForHumanity.org.

Dedication

To my wife and family, who motivate me toward greatness.

To all the great minds of the past that convince us that we, too, can excel.

And for those who have convinced us that:

We are each a direct, reinvented reflection of all those great people who have preceded us and who so positively inspired us to be great.

Contents

Chapter One

What Really Motivates You?

If a blade of grass can grow in a concrete walk and a fig tree in the side of a mountain cliff, a human being empowered with an invincible faith can survive all odds the world can throw against his tortured soul!

—Robert Schuller (b. 1926)
American televangelist, pastor, author

Motivation to do something is a powerful driving force. We know that people have literally done the impossible because they were motivated by some tremendous force. An example of a tremendous driving force that becomes the motivation for non-wavering action is the New York City Marathon. Some thirty-eight thousand marathon runners are fortunate to be selected by a lottery system. Only those selected are eligible to run in the marathon, which is made up of over twenty-six miles of hills and valleys running through the five boroughs of New York City.

So, if approximately forty thousand runners are allowed by lottery to race, how many people request to run each year? In 2008, there were over 105,000 entry forms submitted to the Road Runners Club. I would assume most of the 105,000 entrants were prepared to run the marathon. What type of commitment does it take to prepare for such a grueling race of twenty-six-plus miles? How many weeks, months, or years in advance must the runner practice and exercise for such a long race?

I estimate that a runner would have to practice for at least a year to build up the stamina needed for that distance. Regardless, the entire 105,000 runners requesting entrance were committed to practice and work out and race in the historic marathon. What commitment and drive! The ultimate goal of finishing the New York City Marathon was enough to motivate the runners to get up early before work or to go out late at night to run so many miles in preparation for a marathon that they might or might not have the chance to run in.

Nothing is impossible to a willing mind.

—Monk Hae Chang

What is the motivating force that drives someone to work so hard for a far-off goal? Why do inventors try the impossible when striving to invent something new? An inventor may fail thousands of times before succeeding with a new invention. What sustains his faith in persevering until he has succeeded? Why do some succeed while many more fail?

Well, the way I see it, those who experience repeated failure are often unwilling to go the extra mile that the successful inventor is willing to go. Let's go back to the marathon race. In 2008, there were over thirty-eight thousand actual runners allowed to race. Of the 38,835 at the starting line, the vast majority—37,899 runners—actually finished the 26.2-mile distance. That is commitment. The oldest runner was a man of eighty-seven! He finished the race in eight hours and thirty-nine seconds. Talk about motivation!

To dream anything you want to dream. That's the beauty of the strength of the human mind. To do anything that you want to do. That is the strength of the human will. To trust yourself, to test your limits. That is the courage to succeed.

—Bernard Edmonds, Author

We Are Each Born into This World Destined for Greatness!

Sir George Cayley is considered the father of aerodynamics. In 1800, Cayley was the first person to invent and perfect a glider that was controlled in flight by a human being through the movements of the person's body.

In 1853, fifty years before the first powered flight was made at Kitty Hawk, North Carolina, Cayley built a triplane glider (a glider with three horizontal wing structures) that carried his coachman 900 feet (275 meters) across Brompton Dale in the north of England before crashing. It was the first recorded flight by an adult in an aircraft.

When gliding operators have attained greater skill, they can maintain themselves in the air for hours at a time.

—Wilbur Wright (1867-1912)
Co-inventor of first successful airplane

Every day, in every way, we are each improving on formerly proven and workable ideas, methods, words, and science. And each future generation will continue to improve on our proven and monumental ideas.

I can't help but think of the first cavemen, and how they surely failed and succeeded so many times in their then-short life spans. We truly do live in the best time in the world's history.

Today a former president can have his life saved and extended merely by having fairly routine by-pass surgery performed on his heart. And if need be, his heart can then be re-energized years later by the use of stents to prop open failed arteries. Years ago many of these heart patients simply died for lack of the technology that is readily available today.

A few weeks ago I got the inspiration to try to invent a new way to lift fingerprints off tape—specifically, duct tape. Duct tape is that gray-colored, very heavy, and strong-holding tape that was originally invented to repair aluminum heating air ducts, thus the name duct tape. It also is the tape of choice of many killers. To my knowledge, fingerprints are not easily lifted from the underside of duct tape. But I figured I could find a new way to lift fingerprints. What was my motivation? I was just frustrated with seeing many killers not being brought to justice because the technology of the day lagged in this specific area of forensics.

Now, I didn't really have the time to invest, the knowledge, or the tools needed to invent some new-fangled way of lifting prints, but I had the desire. Of course, I have not succeeded, as of this writing. But I gave it a valiant effort and even surprised myself in my elaborate and extensive experiments in my inventive pursuit. I did not give up, but I have suspended my duct tape experiments for the time being.

My point in this example is this: The inspiration was there. But that intense, never-ending drive was not, at least not at that time. Otherwise, I would never have suspended the experiments, no matter how much failure I encountered.

We learn wisdom from failure much more than from success; we often discover what will do, by finding out what will not do; and probably he who never made a mistake never made a discovery.

—**Samuel Smiles** (1812-1904), Scottish author and reformer

Writing books is much like inventing. A writer undertakes a tremendous endeavor when he plans to write a new book. In the books I have written, I would estimate that it took four to six years per book from the thinking, planning stage until the first printing of the final version. Talk about the need for perseverance and fortitude! There are many times during the writing of a book when doubt sets in. Doubt that I will be able to write enough words, or that it will make sense. Doubt that the readers will like it at all. And doubt that the subject matter is good enough. A seasoned writer can fight through all these negative impulses, realizing that this is normal in the process of writing what you hope will be the best material you have ever written.

But think about maintaining that intense drive for four or six years. And it is an intense drive that motivates a writer to keep picking up that pen, keep writing word after word, even when the words stop flowing. There are times when I sit staring at a blank page, unable to write anything worthwhile. A writer fights through this feeling, this black and negative impulse. In my case, if I can push out even twenty words, I feel better, at least for that moment, knowing that, with time, the flow of words will resume. You see, with an intense desire to finish a book so deeply etched into my subconscious mind, I know the positive impulse to continue writing is ever-present. I will be motivated to continue writing, and also to continue the thinking process that will work through any obstacles I may be facing at that time.

So, a writer who completes a full book has that intense desire to succeed. It is far easier to put the project on hold or just quit when faced with an obstacle that seems insurmountable. And those obstacles are usually many over a four-year period.

For a true writer each book should be a new beginning where he tries again for something that is beyond attainment. He should always try for something that has never been done or that others have tried and failed. Then sometimes, with great luck, he will succeed.

—Ernest Hemingway (1899-1961)
Nobel Prize acceptance speech, American author and journalist

But is it motivation to succeed or a terrible fear of failure? What exactly is it that propels one to the finish line? We will never know whether it is, in fact, fear of failure in some. But to the person who has succeeded it doesn't matter; no one will believe that failure or fear of it had anything to do with her final successful endeavor.

Do what you fear and your fear will die!

—Ralph Waldo Emerson (1803-1882)
American philosopher, essayist, poet

That brings me to something I've been pondering recently: What really motivates us? Do we do great things because we are moved by positive influences, or are we driven by the emotion of fear—the fear of sickness or dying, or the fear of failure? How many great accomplishments might have been the result of actions that grew out of fear?

Recently, I underwent a colonoscopy. Normally, it is a very simple, albeit unpleasant, procedure, but due to a nagging pain I had been experiencing for more than two years, I was highly anxious about the unknown. Add to that fear the fact that a close personal friend had lost his seemingly healthy wife immediately following her first colonoscopy. She was only sixty-two, but she passed away within an hour of completing the test and arriving home. This occurrence placed a brand-new fear deep in my subconscious.

Well, my point is this: I went to the specialist and asked for the colonoscopy because I needed to find out if my worst fear about a possible colon problem was true. I faced up to my fear, or was driven by my fear to positive action, even putting up with fasting from solid food for more than thirty-six hours and drinking over a half-gallon of terrible-tasting solution. I faced my fear of the test itself and what had happened to my friend's wife.

The dreaded test turned out to be a breeze, and the end result was a clean bill of health. Fear was the motivating force behind going for the test that had spooked me for months. So, can great feats come out of fear-driven energy? Can fear of failure or even death result in unbelievable accomplishments? Yes, it's possible that only the person himself will know that the real motivation was fear, even though the outcome was a tremendous positive achievement.

Chapter Two

The Tremendous Motivation
Drawn from Fear

If there is no struggle, there is no progress. Those who profess to favor freedom and yet deprecate agitation ... want crops without plowing up the ground; they want rain without thunder and lightning. They want the ocean without the awful roar of its many waters ... Power concedes nothing without a demand. It never did and it never will.

—**Frederick Douglas** (1817-1895)
American statesman and abolitionist

Now, here is a very important question. I need you to think very carefully about your answer before you respond. If you were in the wilderness, far away from civilization, and you were trapped with your arm stuck between two trees so that you were unable to free yourself, and you were bleeding very heavily, and if the only way you could possibly free yourself was to cut your arm off at the forearm with a pocket knife, could you actually do it?

Think very carefully. You will die for sure if you do nothing. What will you do? Does fear of death actually turn into a tremendous drive to make us forge ahead with the unknown? Is the will to live that powerful? Don't assume here. Don't think that because you may have never done something so drastic before, you couldn't actually perform the act of cutting off your arm in order to live.

It's possible that the person who is typically considered the bravest may not be able to cut his arm off in order to survive, while the most timid, normally unmotivated person may be the first one to act. We never know for sure until we are faced with such a deadly decision whether we would be able to make such a determination. On the one hand, just a few slight slices of the arm's skin may be so excruciating that the act of cutting would actually force you to change your mind. But on the other hand, the thought of leaving your loved ones behind might actually give you the motivation to continue the tedious and excruciating act of cutting off the arm and living. Have you made up your mind? Do you want to live?

The brick walls are there for a reason. Right? The brick walls are not there to keep us out; the brick walls are there to give us a chance to show how badly we want something. Because the brick walls are there to stop the people who don't want it badly enough.

—Randy Pausch (1960-2008)
Professor at Carnegie Mellon University; author of "The Last Lecture"

Breaking through That Brick Wall

Can we each break through that imaginary brick wall, the one that in our minds appears impenetrable? I say *yes*. Each of us can do the unspeakable, the so-called impossible, something neither we nor anyone who knows us intimately would believe us capable of. We may not actually know whether we can accomplish this seemingly impossible action until we are forced to make that tough decision when our backs are flat against the wall.

If you corner a rat, it will attack. If a mother's child is at risk, she will do anything in her power to spare that child. And if that child is pinned under a car, that same mother can lift the car weighing thousands of pounds in order to free her own flesh and blood.

Start by doing what's necessary, then do what's possible, and suddenly you are doing the impossible.

> —**St. Francis of Assisi** (ca. 1181-1226) Catholic deacon and preacher; founder of Franciscan religious order

Here are two examples of the tremendous will to live and what some people can do if their lives are in danger:

On September 11, 2007, Sampson Parker was harvesting corn on his South Carolina farm when his hand got sucked into his old corn picker. As he fought to pull out his gloved hand, the machine's rollers pulled his arm in deeper.

Parker stuck an iron rod into the machine's sprockets to try to slow down the machine's pull on his arm. But instead, this action caused sparks to shoot out and set the ground around him on fire. With his skin melting from the flames, Parker had to make a tough decision: die from the fire spreading around him or cut off his arm and try to escape.

With a pocket knife, he proceeded to cut through his arm and deliberately fell hard to the ground to break through his arm bone, thus severing it from the machine that refused to release it. Parker, with a great loss of blood, proceeded to walk some miles until he was rescued.

Most of the important things in the world have been accomplished by people who have kept on trying when there seemed to be no hope at all.

> —**Dale Carnegie** (1888-1955), American writer and lecturer

While hiking along in Utah's Canyonlands National Park, climber Aron Ralston was descending from a mountain through a three-foot-wide section of the canyon when, suddenly, an eight-hundred-pound boulder shifted and pinned him by his right arm. Unable to free himself for four days, and running out of food and water, Ralston had to make a tough decision. He concluded that he could either try to cut off his arm to free himself, or he would surely die all alone where he was, pinned hopelessly by the huge rock.

So, Ralston proceeded to use a dull pocket knife to cut off his right arm just below the elbow. He thought it out carefully beforehand. Ralston knew that he had to cut his arm at the joint so he could separate it at the elbow. He also knew he needed to minimize blood loss, so he applied his own tourniquet. After severing his arm, Ralston lowered himself approximately sixty feet to the canyon floor and began to walk some five miles to reach his truck.

Finally, Ralston was found when a rescue helicopter that had been alerted to his disappearance spotted him.

When interviewed by *National Geographic Adventure* in August of 2004, Ralston was asked, "But how did someone who had been repulsed by dissecting a sheep's eyeball in ninth-grade science class manage to sever his own hand?"

Ralston answered, "It was strange. I kind of entered a flow state. I've been there before while climbing. You are not thinking ahead. You are just thinking about what is in front of you each second."

Ralston went on to say that the pain was a hundred times worse than anything he had ever felt before.

The courage of life is often a less dramatic spectacle than the courage of a final moment; but it is no less a magnificent mixture of triumph and tragedy. A man does what he must—in spite of personal consequences, in spite of obstacles and dangers and pressures—and that is the basis of all morality.

—**John F. Kennedy** (1917-1963), 35th President of the United States

How Bad Is the Problem That Troubles You?

There are times when we all feel that the world is resting on our shoulders, that our problems are earth-shattering—that is, until we look all around ourselves.

I had the blues because I had no shoes until, upon the street, I met a man who had no feet.

—Ancient Persian saying

We each have felt at some time in our lives that things were the worst they have ever been. Maybe it was because of the loss of personal property of some kind, the theft of a possession such as a car, a wallet, a pocketbook, the loss of our home due to flood or fire. Or maybe it was the loss of our mobility, the inability to walk, broken bones, or sickness of some kind.

Maybe we have terrible throbbing pain, such as back pain, that makes life miserable at times. I don't know about you, but it seems that if I am ever feeling down about myself or my health, I suddenly seem to come across an eye-opening wake-up call. I may be having terrible sciatica pain all day, which can be extremely agonizing. It radiates from the back on down one leg to the toes. Sometimes it happens out of the blue and can be quite bothersome.

It is usually on such a day when I'm feeling slightly sorry for myself that I come across that magical wake-up call. It may be something as simple as an elderly person who is wracked with pain, slowly limping. Or maybe I come across a person who is wheelchair-bound, handicapped, blind, or mentally disabled. I then suddenly, magically, feel fantastic about myself, my body, my aches and pains.

Time and health are two precious assets that we don't recognize and appreciate until they have been depleted.

—Denis Waitley (b. 1933), American motivational speaker, writer

Put It All in Perspective

As I am writing this chapter and listening to the television background noise that we call entertainment, I hear a very troubling story. On an army base in Texas, an army major suddenly snapped and shot two guns, killing twelve people and wounding over thirty more. Once again, it seems like people were in the wrong place at the wrong time. And once again, my back doesn't really hurt anymore. Twelve totally innocent lives. People who woke up just like I did this morning, made breakfast, and got ready for work.

Not once did those dead individuals think that their lives would end that day. It probably didn't cross their minds even once the day before that life is short, that they have much more to accomplish in their lives, and that time is of the essence. We don't really ponder our fate much. We don't really take an accounting of our lives now, or over the past five years, or of what we need to accomplish in the next five years. We all know that life is short. We all know that life is uncertain. But I maintain that we don't act upon this fact very often, that we procrastinate to a large degree, even knowing that we could very well accomplish much more and accomplish it far faster.

Now here is the good news. Look around and find the positives that surround you. As I listen, while writing, to the background press conference about the killings at Fort Hood, Texas, I remember that my uncle will be celebrating his ninety-fifth birthday in a few days. He is in very good shape, very sharp of mind, and still drives his own vehicle all around. He lives alone and cares for himself, as he is a widower. I draw a great deal of inspiration from this 95-year-old man who does not dwell on sickness or death, but merely politely ignores all talk of such things. My uncle would rather discuss whatever is of interest to him at that moment. We all know such older people. We each can draw tremendous inspiration from them.

A boy's will is in his life, and he dies when it is broken, as the colt dies in harness, taking a new nature in becoming tame.

—**Henry Adams** (1838-1918), American journalist, historian, novelist

Count Your Blessings

Each day, count your blessings. Every day, as soon as you open your eyes in the morning, thank God that the gift of a new day has been passed on to you. It is a blessing worth all the gold in the world to have the precious gift of a new and exciting day on earth. No matter whether the day is dark with clouds or pouring down with rain, it is a great day because you are alive. It is a great new opportunity to fix any of yesterday's mistakes and to forge ahead with your present dreams and goals.

We Are Each Born into This World Destined for Greatness!

Elton John, one of the finest musicians of all time, was born Reginald Kenneth Dwight, on March 25, 1947, in England. His father had been a Royal Air Force trumpeter. Elton took up the piano at the age of four and, by age eleven, had won a scholarship to the Royal Academy of Music.

In the 1960s, Elton had already failed at least two auditions for lead singing roles in groups. After answering an ad, he began to team up with a lyricist, Bernie Taupin. Bernie would write the words, and Elton would set the words to music. Elton didn't change any of Bernie's words, which is a pretty amazing thing when writing songs.

Together, Elton and Bernie, writing words and music separately, could put out a song in less than two hours. They began writing songs for a record label, at first for other artists. The first songs that Elton recorded himself were not well-accepted. But within a couple of years, the songwriting duo was pumping out mega-hits. And Elton, the once-rejected lead singer, became the most popular artist of the 1970s.

Elton has put together an amazing career. He has worked through some troubling addictions and turned out to be an amazing success story. In his career, spanning more than four decades, Elton has sold more than 250 million records.

A piano has eighty-eight keys. And we each have the same basic-sounding piano available to us. But among the millions of people who have sat at a piano, Elton makes magic from those thousands of various sound combinations.

Maybe it is talent. Maybe it is love of what we are doing. Maybe it is the intense desire to succeed after failing. Whatever causes it, we are each capable of greatness. And it is important to note that failure almost always precedes great and lasting success.

Chapter Three

Do We Really Appreciate Each New Day?

Never wait on destiny to tap you on the shoulder. You must find it yourself and wrestle it to the ground.

—Marty Lee Parker, Author

I know that everyone says out loud that they appreciate every day they are alive. But I contend that many people don't actually acknowledge each new day as a precious gift from God, rather than something they have a "right" to. Life today is fast and furious. I see people walking and texting on cell phones. As I am at various store counters, I often have to wait while the clerk finishes texting, or as she quickly looks at her cell phone to check the newest text message received since the last one a few seconds earlier.

Others, in an office setting, type on their computers, communicating on Twitter, Facebook, or one of many other social communication sites where much time is wasted and productivity for their employer's business suffers. The mind is working overtime all day, and then into the evening perhaps on the social networking sites at home computers.

I contend that most people don't take the time out daily to be thankful or to do much soul searching. We live today in times very different than in past generations. I remember seeing a video of baseball games from the 1950s and noticing the men dressed in suits and dress hats. I know times have changed, and change is generally good. But I believe we must take time out each day and exercise our minds in a positive-affirmation workout that takes all of five minutes. Let's look at this more closely.

Each and every day, I have a ritual that I do as soon as the alarm goes off. As soon as I open my eyes and acknowledge the time on the clock radio, I say a certain affirmation statement. I have been doing the same ritual for many years, and have progressed to reciting three variations of the statement.

I look out a Palladium window while still in bed, and I repeat the following statement to myself:

"Thank you, Lord, for this new and glorious day. As I look out my window, I see a beautiful blue-white sky with white clouds slowly passing by and colors more brilliant than any picture or painting I've ever seen. I thank you for this new and glorious day. But I don't fully understand why I have been chosen to receive this extra-precious gift of a new day of life while so many others, who were more beneficial to mankind, have been taken away.

"I will not waste this day. I further vow to be kinder and gentler to every single person, no matter who they are or what they may do, because even though it is more difficult to be kinder and gentler to every person, and to lift everyone up rather than tear them down, and to look for the gold rather that the dirt in every person, it's so much more rewarding.

"This will be the finest day of my life, and if I'm fortunate to have a tomorrow, that, too, will be the finest day of my life. I will not let you down, dear Lord; I will not let my family down, but most of all, I will not let myself down. This will be the finest day of my life, and if I'm fortunate to have another, I will fall to my knees and thank you.

"I am the greatest living miracle in the world. I realize that I have not acted like the greatest living miracle in the world, but now I realize that I am, because as the greatest living miracle, I don't worry, because the greatest living miracle realizes that 92 percent of all worry is useless and self-

defeating. The greatest living miracle also doesn't allow fear to get him down, because the greatest living miracle realizes that the Lord is his Shepherd and he shall not fear.

"I vow to act like the greatest living miracle in the world every day for the rest of my life, because I realize now that each and every day I come in contact with many people, and if I begin to act like the greatest living miracle that I am, they will begin to act like the greatest living miracle in the world that they are.

"I thank you for all the precious gifts you have given me through all the years, but most of all I thank you for this extra-precious gift of a new day of life.

"Thank you, Lord. Amen."

That is my early-morning affirmation. I imagine it takes me about three minutes to say the entire statement once straight through, but I admit that I say it very fast. It never changes in order. (And it is much easier to say it than to write it down on paper!)

Why does it work? Remember, all around you every day there are negatives. Bad news on the clock radio, first thing in the morning. Bad news on the way to work as you read the newspaper, and then again on the Internet as soon as the computer connects online.

When we talk about the economy, money, lost jobs, or the latest killer who shoots innocent people, we all discuss the negatives. Why? Because it is just easier to talk about current events and the daily news we are all bombarded with than to talk about more personal things.

So, why not exercise the subconscious mind a few minutes every day? By programming your inner mind, you immunize your mind against the effects of the epidemic of negativity that has sickened so many of our friends and neighbors, making it difficult to advance positively in this world.

Be the change you want to see in the world.

—Mahatma Gandhi (1869-1948),
Political and spiritual leader of India

I did a quick calculation and just surprised myself to realize that I've said my three-minute self-talk affirmations at least twelve thousand times over the past thirty-five years. Remember, when you get into a good habit, anything becomes easier to complete. Anyone can do something for a few days, but when you want to form a new good habit, the task must be completed for twenty consecutive days. So, start off with a small affirmation—something personal to your life, but something, too, that will ward off all the negatives around you.

My affirmations are each etched deep within my subconscious mind. Remember the phrase "Fake it till you make it"? The subconscious is like a young, impressionable child. It will accept whatever you consistently feed it on a daily basis. I feel that my subconscious is just begging for my affirmations. And it is more than cooperative in helping to remind me in my time of need about all the positives I have going on in my life.

You see, I hear all the same terrible, destructive reports, stories, and heartbreaking news stories you hear. The difference, though, is this: The people who exercise their minds with positive affirmations, even small ones, are kept from being completely affected by all the negative influences around them. I hear the conversations of doom and gloom among friends and relatives all the time, but I am able, by my self-training, to allow very, very little of it to penetrate my mind. That is why self-training is so important.

It is a free country. People have the right to vent, complain, and be full of doom and gloom. It's all around them and many people do it. But, like the Olympic athlete, I am fine-tuned and in tip-top shape mentally to put it all in perspective. And in reality, if you want to help yourself in life, you have to put it all in perspective. There's a great little book that makes that point well; it's entitled *Don't Sweat the Small Stuff ... and It's All Small Stuff,* and is by Richard Carlson, Ph.D.

Doom and Gloom

The Great Depression was one of the most discouraging economic times in world history. From 1929 throughout the 1930s, it was the most widespread and devastating period of time for the entire world. People were unemployed in the U.S. to the tune of 25 percent, and some countries had 33 percent unemployment.

There were soup kitchens with long lines of people just happy to have a little bread and a bowl of soup. People were very capable of working, but unable to earn a living because jobs weren't available. As the world eventually started rebounding from the Great Depression, it wasn't long before World War II threatened. Tough times? You bet they were. World War II was the deadliest military conflict in history. It is estimated that the worldwide death toll from that war was around seventy million—both from fighting and from war-related diseases.

So, we have always been affected by doom and gloom. Still, people thrive, even in the face of disasters. Keep it all in perspective.

Some Things Never Change

In a very old book I picked up while on vacation in Ireland, *The Recreations of a Country Parson*, published around 1863 in Scotland, a pastor in a small Scottish community discusses his life and times. I am very impressed by the simplicity of things and by the appreciation of little things such as ". . . a sunshiny day, a mossy green carefully mown lawn, lilacs, oak, horse-chestnut and hawthorn trees, a horse, a stable and a pig."

This religious man appreciates all of the little things while preparing text for his Sunday sermons at his little parish church. He talks about horse carriage rides of some distance to catch a train that will carry him some one hundred fifty miles on a weeklong holiday. I suddenly think about our cell phones that allow us to speak across the globe in a split-second from anywhere we may be. I think about our Internet that allows us to conduct in mere seconds vast amounts of research that would otherwise take us weeks to uncover. I realize that now we can prepare foods in minutes that would have taken all day to prepare in the 1860s. Still, the parson's life holds an attraction we may never know, a simplicity we have totally lost in our 300-mile-per-hour world that appears to be going even faster every day.

In the book, the author explains some of the principles the people held dear in 1860—principles we should still hold dear today, even though their lives differed so much from ours. As I read, I thought about life with no radio, television, cars, planes, ATMs, or Starbucks. And once again, I ask: Do we really appreciate the life with which we've been blessed?

A passage of the book reads:

I have been writing down some thoughts, as I have said, for the sermon of next Sunday. Tomorrow morning I shall begin to write it fully out. Some individuals, I am aware, have maintained that listening to a sermon is irksome work; but to a man whose tastes lie in that way, the writing of sermons is most pleasant occupation. It does you good. Unless you are a mere false pretender, you cannot try to impress any truth forcibly upon the hearts of others without impressing it forcibly upon your own. All that you will ever make other men feel will be only a subdued reflection of what you yourself have felt. And sermon-writing is a task that is divided into many stages. You begin afresh every week; you come to an end every week. If you are writing a book, the end appears very far away. If you find that although you do your best, you yet treat some part of your subject badly, you know that the bad passage remains as a permanent blot: and you work on under the cross-influence of that recollection. But if, with all your pains, this week's sermon is poor, why, you hope to do better next week. You seek a fresh field: you try again.

—Andrew Kennedy Hutchison Boyd

That passage was written some one hundred forty-five years ago. As much as things change, and they do change at the very rapid speed of light, things also remain the same—emotions, the need to put one's mark on some respected work, the need to help someone who needs something, and the desire to be remembered for many years after having passed on.

The parson's words have reminded me of how I wish to touch at least one person's life deeply with the ideas and words I have passed along. One life. One person who will move forward and who, in turn, will touch another person's life. That is what life is all about.

The Wisdom We Gain with Age

In Mitch Albom's insightful book *Tuesdays with Morrie*, we encounter a 78-year-old professor, Morrie, dealing with the death sentence he faces as he slowly succumbs to the ravages of ALS (Lou Gehrig's disease). We learn from a genius of a man who explains life and its wonders to us as he faces death with dignity.

In the following excerpt from the book, Morrie is asked about dealing with growing old:

Weren't you ever afraid to grow old, I asked.

"Mitch, I embrace aging."

Embrace it?

"It's very simple. As you grow, you learn more. If you stayed at twenty-two, you'd always be as ignorant as you were at twenty-two. Aging is not just decay, you know. It's growth. It's also the positive that you understand you're going to die, and that you live a better life because of it."

Yes, I said, but if aging were so valuable, why do people always say, "Oh, if I were young again." You never hear people say, "I wish I were sixty-five."

He smiled. "You know what that reflects? Unsatisfied lives. Lives that haven't found meaning. Because if you've found meaning in your life, you don't want to go back. You want to go forward. You want to see more, do more. You can't wait until sixty-five."

Perhaps Morrie was looking forward to the hereafter, a new chapter in growth for a professor who had touched so many lives. And even in death, Morrie's story touched millions, both through the written word and on the big screen in the movie *Tuesdays with Morrie*. What a brave person Morrie was. At the lowest point of his life, when each part of his body was rapidly shutting down, he was still giving lessons on life and on how to look upon death with fresh eyes. His death was a great loss for those still living. But Morrie finally graduated to a new and exciting adventure still to play out.

I have often thought that the best way to define a man's character would be to seek out the particular mental or moral attitude in which, when it came upon him, he felt himself most deeply and intensely active and alive. At such moments, there is a voice inside which speaks and says: "This is the real me!"

—**William James** (1842-1910),
American philosopher and psychologist

We Are Each Born into This World Destined for Greatness!

Doctor R. T. H. Laennec invented the world's first stethoscope.

One day in 1816, Dr. Laennec was invited by urchins to hear the scratching of a pin, transmitted through the length of a wooden beam. Dr. Laennec was then inspired to fashion a paper tube to listen to the chest of his patients—thus, the first stethoscope.

We each have the ability, deep inside, to achieve greatness. It may be a simple invention, or the monumental improvement on a past invention, that leaves us even more successful than the original inventor. The point here is: never take your inner greatness for granted.

Make no little plans. They have no magic to stir men's blood and probably themselves will not be realized. Make big plans. Aim high in hope and work. Remembering that a noble, logical diagram once recorded will not die.

—Daniel H. Burnham (1846-1912), Architect and urban planner

Chapter Four

Motivation in Times of Despair

As I write, we are facing tough economic conditions in America. Many people are out of work. So how does one find inspiration in depressing times? What do you tell a person who can't find a job, though he is willing and able to work? Despair can be devastating to someone who has no place to turn.

There may be a job opening that draws hundreds of applicants. How can you compete against hundreds of résumés? There are surely better résumés than yours amidst the staggering competition of hundreds of other applicants.

My only answer is: creativity. Be different. Use your imagination to stand out from the crowd. Maybe you can take out an ad in the help-wanted section of the newspaper. Maybe you can do research on the firm at which you are applying and make a booklet, including their history, photos, and bullet points of why you specifically want to work for them.

Maybe you can be bold enough to write up a contract spelling out, on top of all other things, that you will work for the firm for one, two, or three months for no wages, as long as, after that time frame, you will be considered first out of all other résumés for the full-time position.

This system has been used similarly in temporary positions where the temp job becomes full-time and is filled by the person who held the part-time position.

Be different! Be unique! Stand out from the crowd! Tough times call for tough-thinking people who are bold enough to make a difference. It is easy to follow the crowd. But go-getters will always find ways to succeed, even in tough times.

Aim at perfection in everything, though in most things it is unattainable. However, they who aim at it, and persevere, will come much nearer to it than those whose laziness and despondency make them give it up as unattainable.

—**Lord Chesterfield** (1694-1773), British statesman

We Are Each Born into This World Destined for Greatness!

Bette Nesmith's name may not ring a bell with you. But the Nesmith name does sound familiar to many in the music business. Michael Nesmith was one of The Monkees in the popular television series, and the band recorded many hit songs.

But Bette, Michael's mother, went down in history in the office supply business and in offices around the world. Bette invented the "Liquid Paper" correction fluid in a bottle in 1956.

Bette had always wanted to be an artist. Instead, she was an executive secretary in Dallas, as well as a single parent. She used her own kitchen blender to mix up the first batch of Liquid Paper. She concluded that a painter would cover mistakes in his paintings with a certain type of paint, so why not fix typing errors in a similar manner? So, in 1956, Bette invented and perfected the formula, and the rest is history. A unique idea to solve an everyday problem. Why did it take so long for someone to fix such a common problem?

We all have greatness deep within. If one is determined with all his heart, that greatness will indeed find a way to come out into the open. What are you fired up about? What is the first thing you think about in the morning and the last thing you think about each and every night?

You can create such an intense desire, even if none currently exists. But just like all greatness achieved by others in the past, you must carefully plan out and devise such an elaborate goal that you will hang on right till the end. Remember, you must always focus on the *finish line*!

The Amazing Miracle of Life

I have always been amazed at the amazing miracle of life. If anyone believes that any form of life is anything but a true miracle, he should do some serious research into the subject. I appreciate the life with which I have been blessed; I have for many years. But, honestly, when I was very young, the miracle of life all around me meant very little. I didn't give it a second thought. Now, as I look all around in my middle age, I look at life, the world, and the stars entirely differently. It all amazes me.

Life exists in many forms, from plants and blades of grass to insects and microscopic organisms. Some say the smallest organism that exists is a form of virus. I, on the other hand, understand what I can see. There are insects so small they are called fairy flies at one-fifth of a millimeter in size. They have a respiratory system, wings, and microscopic hairs on their bodies.

My point is this: Life is so precious; do we maximize our own existence, or do some of us merely pass our lives away, thinking that time is on our side and we can always catch up to our goals and dreams that have been put off indefinitely?

Earl Nightingale, the motivational speaker and author, once said: "Most people tiptoe through life, hoping to make it safely to death."

Stop Taking Up Space—Start Making a Difference

What is our purpose here on earth? Do we have a purpose, and do all living organisms serve some purpose? Let's explore it more closely.

Last night I found a snail. No big deal. But I found the snail attached to the inside of an electric timer inside a large plastic storage bin. Now, what was amazing to me was that the storage bin had been closed for one year, only accessed last Christmastime, some twelve months ago. Yet, when I opened it up, there was a live snail. The miracle of life! I wondered how that snail, deep inside the large storage bin, could have survived. What did it eat and drink? And surviving in total darkness! Now, I am sure that there is some explanation, but I simply marvel at the perseverance and survival instinct of all living things.

What is the purpose of it all? From the moment of birth, each form of life has a purpose, a pre-programmed cycle we must follow, much like the cycles of seasons that change. Most living things have inbred cycles of routines and schedules. Take, for instance, the cicada. The cicada is an insect that lives approximately one to eight feet underground and emerges only once every seventeen years. When they do emerge, many thousands of them emerge at the same time, resulting in a great deal of noise. Purpose, cycle, routine!

We are much like insects. I believe that we act like insects. Take the ant. An ant farm is very organized, with leaders and workers, each with a purpose and a structured life cycle. Our lives, in many ways, seem to mirror some of nature. It is important for us to be cognizant of this so we may be able to adjust our lives accordingly, and strive onward where others may merely be complacent.

I am here for a purpose and that purpose is to grow into a mountain, not to shrink to a grain of sand. Henceforth I will apply ALL my efforts to become the highest mountain of all and I will strain my potential until it cries for mercy.

—Og Mandino (1923-1996), American motivational author

How many individuals do only what they have to, just to get to the next day? Their workday is basically performing tasks they are told to do and no more. They treat work like some form of punishment, just to survive till that clock hits five o'clock, telling them that they can rush out the door and race home. Not once do they act as if the company they are working for is theirs. Many workers today have little pride in their work. I see it many times throughout my day and in my travels. Maybe this is because they have no real goal to get ahead or rise above the average workers around them. Maybe they have no long-term goals, no intense, burning desire with regard to the work they are involved in. Or maybe they dislike their line of work, just tolerating it in exchange for a paycheck.

I observe many people that are being well paid to work all day, yet I see them loafing. It's as if they are impatiently waiting to go home. They are cheating their employer, themselves, their families, and, above all, their God. Just another wasted day, being unproductive.

Martin Luther King said it best: "If a man is called to be a street sweeper, he should sweep streets even as Michelangelo painted, or Beethoven composed music, or Shakespeare wrote poetry. He should sweep streets so well that all the hosts of Heaven and earth will pause to say here lived a great street sweeper who did his job well."

Make every minute of your life count. Make believe that tomorrow you will cease to be productive any longer, but rather will ponder your life. Will you be proud or disappointed? You have the ability to drastically change that picture. Remember: This is the first day of the rest of your new and exciting life. Embrace, cherish, and celebrate the special gift of that one day.

A man should conceive of a legitimate purpose in his heart, and set out to accomplish it. He should make this purpose the centralizing point of his thoughts. It may take the form of a spiritual ideal, or it may be a worldly object, according to his nature at the time being; but whichever it is, he should steadily focus his thought forces upon the object which he has set before him. He should make this purpose his supreme duty, not allowing his thoughts to wander away into ephemeral fancies, longings, and imaginings. This is the royal road to self-control and true concentration of thought. Even if he fails again and again to accomplish his purpose (as he necessarily must until weakness is overcome), the strength of character gained will be the

measure of his true success, and this will form a new starting point for future
power and triumph.

—**James Allen** (1864-1912), British author

Perseverance Means Never Giving Up

It is amazing to me how many people just naturally take to following other people. It is as if it is easier to follow along than to travel their own road. This morning this "following the follower" came to mind when I saw a flock of birds.

Nature has a way of preserving animals, birds, and other forms of life. We see elephants, seals, penguins, birds, and the ape family. There is the leader who makes choices as to where to seek water, food, and shelter. The leader also moves the flock or herd to safer territory or different climates.

This morning I studied a large flock of blackbirds flying in precision formation as they swooped from one lawn to another. They were eating either some of the grass seed or some bugs on the ground. But what was amazing was that, as soon as the leader decided to fly away from a particular lawn, the entire flock followed rapidly, wherever the leader flew.

I find that many people are like that. Maybe it is bred into us from nature or instinct alone, but many of us would like to merely follow rather than lead the way.

Of course, there are those special people who are called "born leaders." What is a born leader anyway? Inventors could be considered born leaders because they travel down roads that were never traveled before. Inventors work on the nearly impossible. They are fearless leaders. Inventors don't get thrown by all the negative criticism they receive. The inventor merely trudges along after each failure, knowing in their hearts that success will surely present itself in a future experiment.

So, why can't most of us lead rather than follow? I guess it is too easy just to take the road well-traveled rather than cut your own way through the forest and blaze a new trail. We were each created to be born leaders, but somewhere along the way we became weak, and then naturally fell in line behind the braver, tougher, natural leader.

Today, this special day, let us use our imagination. Let us make believe that we are an inventor such as Thomas Edison. And during this experiment let us each do something new, challenging, and almost impossible. Let us become the inventor of our own life. Maybe we can emulate that persevering mindset of the great inventor for an entire week! You will be shocked at how you attack work and life like the inventor you have imagined yourself to be.

In the wild, the strongest ape is the leader. The males routinely fight among themselves to determine the leader. The leader in most species is tested regularly, until one day he becomes too weak to lead.

I believe that we were born to be great leaders, each one of us. But perhaps our upbringing, nurturing, relationships as youngsters, the crowd we hung out with in school, our slowly formed personalities, all contributed to who we evolved into as adults. Some of us take chances without fear of failing because our confidence level is high, while others fear confrontation, fear risks, and are more comfortable taking a sure route that we know we can conquer. Thus, we follow the follower.

Inventors have the key to achieving goals. Successful authors, business owners, and athletes all have the key. They have figured out how to program their minds with this special, never-ending, burning desire to succeed in their dream goal. They may not even be aware of what it is that they have done within themselves to achieve the outcomes they so desperately desired. But they have actually etched deeply into their subconscious minds the burning desire to achieve that special goal.

It may be a youngster who has a huge dream of becoming a Major League Baseball player. He dreams of playing in the Major Leagues, like his baseball idols such as Derek Jeter. He sees Derek Jeter for years playing baseball as one of the best who ever played the game, and the youngster slowly develops the intense desire to emulate Jeter. The desire gets etched deeply into the youngster's subconscious mind, and just as he unconsciously blinks his eyes and breathes the air he needs to survive, the intense desire to succeed keeps radiating like a flashing sign, all on its own, pushing the youngster to the ultimate dream of success.

We each have had smaller goals that were intensely driven desires upon which we acted until they were fulfilled. Let's look at such a goal. Perhaps in our youth we watched with great enjoyment the television program *ER*. As we watched show after show, we slowly developed a consuming goal to become a great doctor like the ones we so admired on the show. We became obsessed with becoming that doctor, or that nurse. Or maybe we were influenced by another show to become a great lawyer. Because of the intense desire now deeply etched into our subconscious mind, we are motivated to seek higher education and a degree in order to fulfill this all-consuming dream. Will we be millionaires, insanely rich? Perhaps. In Og Mandino's fabulous self-help book *The Greatest Salesman in the World*, he talks about changing the way we think by feeding certain statements into our minds. He talks about controlling emotions when he says:

> *I will be master of my emotions. If I feel depressed, I will sing. If I feel sad, I will laugh. If I feel ill, I will double my labor. If I feel fear, I will plunge ahead. If I feel inferior, I will wear new garments. If I feel uncertain, I will raise my voice. If I feel poverty, I will think of wealth to come. If I feel incompetent, I will remember past success. If I feel insignificant, I will remember my goals. Today I will be the master of my emotions.*

The Power of Belief

The mind is so powerful that if we could harness its immense capabilities, we could run an entire state's computer system. Our mind, if programmed properly, will bring forth to its owner an abundance of wealth, fame, love, success, and anything that is truly desired. The key is that the desire should be so strong that nothing in the world will stop that person from attaining the goal or dream that has so driven her to the desired end.

I believe with all my heart that if we could somehow program a person's brain on a systematic basis—that is, a formal program that would feed that person's brain a set of thoughts, almost like hypnosis—then we could control the outcome of that person's life and actions. The key is that the programming must be done consistently. We would have to take that person in each week and reprogram those same thoughts. Could it work? Yes, I believe it could work.

So, let us study successful outcomes. If I develop not only my own dreams and goals but, more important, a tremendous, never-ending, all-consuming, burning desire, that is the outcome that will be achieved. At that moment, there will be a newfound glow all about me; my face, my demeanor, my stride will even be different. And guess what? My pain is almost gone!

You see what I mean? Our subconscious mind can be rewired and programmed with new and positive thought impulses that can overtake any negatives that may have been affecting us for some time.

If you can understand that the mind controls not only the body but most of your actions, and will be responsible ultimately for the outcomes in your life, you will try to control what is being put into that amazing computer of a mind that we don't even fully understand.

The opposite, negative impulse is also true. The phone rings and you learn that your mother suddenly had a massive stroke, or fell and broke a hip and will have to have major hip replacement surgery as soon as possible. Feel the sudden impulses? Or what if you suddenly receive a call and find that you just landed a great new job after more than a year of being unemployed? What are the impulses now? How long will they last? Notice how our minds can suddenly be turned three hundred sixty degrees from positive to negative and then from negative to positive again.

What about a cancer diagnosis? Doctor Bernie Siegel has his own thoughts on attitudinal thinking. Doctor Siegel is a clinical professor of surgery at Yale Medical School. He has said:

I have collected fifty-seven extremely well-documented so-called cancer miracles. A cancer miracle is when a person didn't die when he absolutely, positively was supposed to. At a certain particular moment in time, he decided that the anger and the depression were probably not the best way to go, since he had such a little bit of time left, and so he went from that state to being loving, caring, no longer angry, no longer depressed, and able to talk to the people he loved. These fifty-seven people had the same pattern. They gave up totally their anger, and they gave up totally their depression by specifically making a decision to do so. And at that point the tumors started to shrink.

Does the mind really control the body? You bet it does. When the will to live dies, the person usually dies a short time later. How many spouses die within a couple of months or years of losing their spouse? The human body will obey the commands given by the all-powerful mind. So watch what you feed your mind. Put it all in perspective: There are people with no money, but others with money but no life left to live—perhaps only days. There are those who have to walk with a cane, but there are those who are wheelchair-bound for life. Then there are people who are deaf, but there are also those who have been blind since birth. Perspective is very important.

In 1954, Roger Banister proved everyone wrong when he ran a one-mile distance in under four minutes. No one up to that point had ever done it. Banister trained hard and long to achieve this. But here's an important point: Within one year, thirty-seven other runners broke the four-minute mile. And after that, three hundred others did it, too.

You see, once others were convinced that the four-minute mile could, in fact, be broken, they worked harder, knowing that they, too, could do it because it had finally been demonstrated that it was humanly possible.

Since the human body tends to move in the direction of its expectations, plus or minus, it is important to know that attitudes of confidence and determination are no less a part of the treatment program than medical science and technology

—Norman Cousins (1915-1990), Author, professor

Remember the story of the man who felt bad because he had no shoes, until he came across a man who had no feet? We need to take a full accounting each and every day. We need to thank God that we have been blessed with another day to experience life on earth. Be thankful for what you do have, but really add it all up, item by item, sense by sense. Then you will really appreciate all you have going for you.

Chapter Five

Thinking Differently Leads to Success

It is our thinking more than anything else that will determine our long-term success, or our "flash-in-the-pan," short-term success. It was once said of Elvis Presley in the very beginning of his career that he was nothing more than "a flash in the pan." Well, for a flash in the pan, this man went on to become the King of Rock and Roll. Elvis's records have sold over one billion copies, and in 2009, his estate earned $50 million in all marketing efforts. There is even a radio station, Sirius Satellite radio, that plays 100 percent Elvis Presley songs 24/7.

The problem with some people is that they have no vision or imagination. When they see or experience something unique, they can't visualize it working long-term. Some people are in a mental rut; they have no problem accepting all the amazing improvements in technology, but they don't want to modify their own thinking to improve their position in the world. Leo Tolstoy said, "Everyone thinks of changing the world, but no one thinks of changing himself." And British politician Harold Wilson put it this way: "He who rejects change is the architect of decay. The only human institution which rejects progress is the cemetery."

What do you think about all day? Sometimes our minds get stuck in a bad mode. Let me explain what mode I am talking about. We have all been guilty of negative thinking at some time in our lives. It may be when we are not feeling 100 percent healthy. Maybe it is our teeth that hurt, like a bad cavity that needs to be drilled and crowned. Or it could be our back that suddenly goes out again or goes out for the first time. Just like the signals of pain that radiate from the defective tooth or bad disk in the back, the brain is constantly producing signals of positive or negative thoughts. These impulses affect the ultimate outcome of our efforts. Good impulses result in good outcomes; bad impulses will give you terrible outcomes.

We can control our lives by controlling the impulses our mind sends out every split second. And it literally is every split second that your subconscious mind is sending these thought impulses to your conscious mind. Thus, our subconscious mind, which works always in the background, is silently controlling our actions and our moods and, more importantly, advertising to everyone all around us exactly how we feel.

It has been estimated that the average human brain thinks of some sixty thousand thoughts per day. Positive affirmations will keep some of those negative thoughts that surround us under control.

The happiness of your life depends upon the quality of your thoughts ... take care that you entertain no notions unsuitable to virtue and reasonable nature.

—Marcus Aurelius (121-180), Roman emperor

We may find ourselves in that mental rut. It could be the aches in our body. It could be the fact that we have arrived at middle age, or the lack of money in our pockets, or the fact that we are unemployed and can't locate another job. But here is an important point: Our minds can be reprogrammed midstream. Even though we may be in a negative subconscious-mode for days or weeks, we can at any given point rewire those thought impulses into very positive impulses. And those new impulses can last days, weeks, or months. Let's look at this fact more closely.

My back is aching, and my bad knee that was operated on for torn cartilage is hurting with each step; both have been hurting for days. Suddenly, my phone rings and my sister tells me that my only niece has just announced she is engaged to be married a year from now. What is my thought process at this very moment?

Or my mother suddenly calls and informs me that my younger sister who was married three years earlier is now pregnant with her first child and that I am going to be a first-time uncle. Oh, and yes, my sister is going to ask my wife and me to be the baby's godparents. What impulses are suddenly being generated by that all-powerful part of my mind, the subconscious? The euphoria I suddenly feel is overwhelming and will last for a long time.

What if my brother suddenly called and informed me that he just hit the Mega Millions Lottery for $25 million? And he also informed the entire family that he would be paying off all of their outstanding loans, including their mortgages—what is my mindset now?

Can we go from feeling troubled to feeling euphoric in just a split second? On the other hand, can we shift and feel tremendously depressed in that same split-second time frame? Of course we can. But knowing how our minds respond to outside stimuli should convince us that we are in many ways in full control of turning our attitudes around. That sadness and depression can be turned around fairly rapidly with some specific and pointed effort. We must, therefore, understand more about this powerful mind that controls our bodies every second we are alive. We are in control. We are each capable of maintaining long-term happiness and positive attitudes. But we must each make that conscious, ongoing effort to learn, to practice motivating ourselves, and to maintain that positive effort which can last our whole lifetime.

Remember: sixty thousand thoughts per day. We exercise the muscles of our body, why not practice daily to exercise our mind with personalized positive affirmations?

The Destructive Trait of Worry

Ninety percent of worry is considered by the experts to be needless. Some people are consumed with worry.

They may worry about their health, the health of their loved ones, or just nonsense that others may believe to be foolish. Worry can consume a person's life, drain their energy, and weaken the immune system, causing a person to get sick more easily.

Worry can infect almost anyone at any time. But if I find myself worrying needlessly, I ask myself, "Do I have control over this situation? Can I change the outcome? Then forget about it!" That's right. I tell myself, "Forget about it!" As soon as the words are spoken, a certain feeling of relief sets in. You can also say, "And this, too, shall pass."

The realization that the outcome of the situation is out of my control relieves the tension. There is a great statement that puts it all into perspective:

> *Things We Worry About*
> *Things that never happen: 40%.*
> *Things over and past, that can't be changed: 30%.*
> *Needless worries about our health: 12%.*
> *Petty, miscellaneous worries: 10%.*
> *Real legitimate worries: 8%*
> *Which leaves 92 percent of all worry we do as useless.*
> —**Dr. Walter Cavert**

We all have a variety of worries and fears as we go through life: fear of not marrying the right person, of failing in business, of dying, of the loss of a loved one, of being poor, and thousands of other fears.

You can control your fears by using these techniques:

1. Put the fear in proper perspective.
2. Analyze the fear. Why are you worrying?

3. What is the worst possible thing that could happen? If the worst possible thing does happen, will you still have your mind? Will you still be alive? How terrible will it really be? In reality, how terribly important is this thing that worries you?

4. Write out the worst possible scenario on paper, then remind yourself that 92 percent of all worrying is not necessary.

We Are Each Born into This World Destined for Greatness!

The true measure of a person's success in life should not be judged by their rise to wealth or stature, but rather by the degree to which they have positively influenced other lives in their own lifetime.

—JPC

Born in Sharon, Pennsylvania, John D. MacDonald wished, as a young boy, that he had been born a writer, believing that writers were a separate "race," marked somehow from birth. By the time he died, he had published seventy-eight books with more than 75 million copies in print. He wrote nearly five hundred short stories and published his first novel, *The Brass Cupcake*, in 1950. John MacDonald passed on in 1986 at the early age of 70, but he continues to earn praise from millions of readers and lasting respect from fellow authors.

I remember writing my own very first novel years ago. It took me five years to complete it. And my first self-help book took fifteen years until it was in print. It is difficult to comprehend one person writing seventy-eight books.

MacDonald served as a real influence in my writing of novels. He wrote in the first-person style, and his fiction was very visual and believable. I tried to emulate him. I wonder how many other first-time authors have been inspired by him in their writing careers.

MacDonald's books are still being sold today, over sixty years after he published his first book. You see, we can each evolve into greatness. We can each touch many thousands of lives positively in our own lifetime. Just as the air we breathe infiltrates our bodies, so, too, can a well-written book infect us, if we allow it to, with the never-ending inspiration to excel in our own lives.

MacDonald once said, "Integrity is not a conditional word. It doesn't blow in the wind or change with the weather. It is your inner image of yourself, and if you look in there and see a man who won't cheat, then you know he never will."

Chapter Six

Your Powerful Mind

Each person comes into this world with a specific destiny—he has something to fulfill, some message has to be delivered, some work has to be completed. You are not here accidentally—you are here meaningfully. There is a purpose behind you. The whole intends to do something through you.

—Osho (1931-1990), Indian mystic

The human mind is so powerful that we still don't understand exactly how it works, and most of us don't realize all the ways the mind controls the body. It has been noted that, the human brain, if measured in a certain capacity, could store more than three million hours of video.

It is psychological law that whatever we desire to accomplish we must impress upon the subjective or subconscious mind.

—Orison Swett Marden (1850-1924),
American writer and founder of *Success* magazine

The subconscious mind, if maximized, can catapult you and your career to heights previously unimaginable. The trick lies in understanding how this inner part of the mind, which is always working silently in the background, can be fed special instructions which will program it. If programmed properly, the subconscious will feed the conscious part of your mind continuously and almost unbeknownst to you while you are sleeping, watching television, walking, working, or eating. The subconscious is like a power plant all in itself that can power up the body to accomplish what it could not otherwise do.

In a very insightful book by Joseph Murphy, Ph.D., D.D., entitled *The Power of Your Subconscious Mind*, he delves into the working of the subconscious:

The power of your subconscious is beyond all measure. It inspires you and guides you. It calls up vivid scenes from the storehouse of memory. Your subconscious controls your heartbeat and the circulation of your blood. It regulates your digestion, assimilation, and elimination. When you eat a piece of bread, your subconscious mind transmutes it into tissue, muscle, bone, and blood. These processes are beyond the ken of the wisest person who walks the earth. Your subconscious mind controls all the vital processes and functions of your body. It knows the answer to all the problems.

Your subconscious mind never sleeps, never rests. It is always on the job. You can discover the miracle-working power of your subconscious by plainly stating to your subconscious, prior to sleep, that you want a specific thing accomplished.

It is foolish to believe in sickness and something to hurt or to harm you. Believe in perfect health, prosperity, peace, wealth, and divine guidance.

—**Joseph Murphy** (1898-1981), Divine Science minister and author

A very useful tool built into the subconscious mind shows itself when you ask it to work on a problem. When writing novels, there are times when I have been stuck in limbo with a story that needs something more to move it ahead. Or sometimes I have a special problem in business that I can't seem to work out. In these times, I merely put before my subconscious in very direct and urgent terms the questions or the task I need to be worked on. And then I go about my business as usual.

I have been awakened from a very sound sleep on many occasions and at all times of the night, and suddenly have been given complete and detailed resolutions to the troubling business problems I had previously thought unsolvable. I have also been given, at these special enlightening times, complete story lines or, in certain instances, the ending to a story that I had not been able to finish. I have been given invention ideas and many business solutions. This is a special tool that anyone can utilize.

It makes good sense to keep a pad and pen on your nightstand at all times because, once you begin to give instructions to your subconscious mind, it will pick the oddest times to flood your mind with the answers you had been seeking all along.

Remember that the subconscious mind will accept whatever is being fed into it on a constant basis. Be very careful what you routinely think about and what influences you allow to penetrate this most powerful part of your mind. In other words, the subconscious will accept fact or fiction that is consistently passed into it through our conscious thoughts. Therefore, if I were to repeat a series of positive statements, or *affirmations*, as they are often called, they would be absorbed and accepted.

Here is a series of affirmation statements that, if said periodically throughout the day, will have positive results in your life within a few weeks. These statements should be customized to fit your particular situation. But here are some that I often use:

"I feel healthy, I feel happy, I feel terrific!"

"I like myself! I like myself! I like myself!"

"I will be successful; it's inevitable because my aggressiveness will lead to my success!"

You see, once the subconscious hears, understands, and accepts the positive statements, it understands that you have just programmed it so that it will work, without your knowledge (*subconsciously*—below the level of your consciousness), to send these positive statements or vibes back out to the conscious mind throughout your working day and even while you sleep.

But be careful, because the subconscious is like an obedient servant. It wants to please its master or mistress. Therefore, it will also readily accept negative statements and thoughts as factual, and as programming instructions. In turn, it will release these negative impulses out to the conscious mind consistently.

It is a well-known rule that habits are formed in about twenty days. You can break a bad habit or form a new good habit in three weeks' time. So, if you want to stop smoking, that habit can be broken by doing without cigarettes for three weeks. Easier said than done, I know. But by utilizing positive affirmations, the bad habit can fall by the wayside. Here are a few such statements to try:

"Stop smoking! Stop!"

"Stop ruining your lungs!"

"Stop! I have so much to live for! I'm killing myself!"

"Stop! You can't do this!"

Formulate and stamp indelibly on your mind a mental picture of yourself as succeeding. Hold this picture tenaciously and never permit it to fade. Your mind will seek to develop this picture!

—**Dr. Norman Vincent Peale** (1898-1993),
Protestant preacher and author

It is a psychological law that whatever we wish to accomplish we must impress on the subjective or subconscious mind.

—**Orison Swett Marden** (1850-1924), American writer;
founder of *Success* magazine

An All-Consuming Desire

Now that we understand how powerful the subconscious mind is, and how it can change your life for the better, or for the worse if programmed negatively, let us look at some examples.

Chesley B. Sullenberger III is the famed pilot of U.S. Airways Flight 549, which he miraculously crash-landed in New York City's Hudson River on Thursday, January 15, 2009. As a child, Sullenberger had a very high IQ that even qualified him for the "genius society" Mensa at the age of twelve.

When we study the man, we learn that Sullenberger's father took his own life. This, no doubt, had a profound impact on the value Sullenberger placed on human life. Perhaps Sullenberger treated his passengers' lives more carefully because of his father's suicide.

Starting at age nine, Sullenberger had desired to become a pilot, and beginning at age sixteen, he took lessons from a crop-duster pilot. He continued this flight training in the military. It is apparent that Sullenberger etched the dream of flying planes deep into his subconscious mind from a very young age. Sullenberger clearly is a driven man. It is this intense desire that has inspired the man to push on and become one of the best in his field.

Success is a by-product of sheer determination and hard work. It's as if the subconscious has been so intensely programmed that it somehow supercharges the conscious mind and body on a regular basis, and this is what carries the person across the finish line of any all-consuming desire. It was Sullenberger who said, "We need to try to do the right thing every time, to perform at our best because we never know at what moment in our lives we will be judged."

Trust yourself. Create the kind of life you will be happy to live with all of your life. Make the most of yourself by fanning the tiny inner sparks of possibility into the flames of achievement.

—**Foster C. McClellan,** Author

Decide what it is that you want to achieve. Write it out in full detail. Tape Post-Its with the name of the goal all over your home and workplace. Tell everyone what it is that you intend to accomplish. Be proud of your goal. But most of all, concentrate each morning, noon, and night on the achievement of the goal or task. Always focus on the finish line. As you work through all the obstacles and pitfalls you encounter, see the finish line, the completion, the award ceremony you will have in your mind when you reach the finish line.

Any marathon runner or bike racer or Olympic athlete must focus on the finish line. They must keep the cobwebs out, go through their routine endless times. They visualize their technique and what to avoid along the way. In other words, they psych themselves up or motivate themselves. The true sign of a winner is that they expect to win. Many winners never once think of failure or that they might not succeed.

Inventors are the most driven individuals because they must do the seemingly impossible. They invent something or improve something in a manner that hasn't been done before. All along the way the inventor experiences failed attempts. Sometimes those failed attempts number in the thousands, but that doesn't deter the inventor. He welcomes failure, realizing that each new failure brings him closer to his breakthrough, the successful completion of the invention.

Salespeople work the same way. Each "no" they receive brings them that much closer to their "yes," their sale. They are not discouraged by someone's refusal to buy because they know that they must maintain that all-powerful positive attitude; otherwise, the sales will never come.

So, it is important to maintain that winning attitude no matter how rough the road to the goal. It is important to use positive affirmations to remind the mind, to psych up the mind, so no negative impulses will jeopardize or get in the way of that finish line, that award ceremony you will have at the time of your achievement.

Whether the goal or task is small or large, the concept and method are the same. In fact, I recommend right this minute that you come up with three very small tasks. Write them down, but do only one at a time. Celebrate each small victory in your mind. Once you achieve the third goal, it will be time to choose bigger, longer-term tasks, dreams, goals. But you will be confident that the system works and that you are capable of reaching each finish line.

Og Mandino, in his book *The Greatest Salesman in the World,* uses positive affirmations such as this:

I will persist until I succeed. The prizes of life are at the end of each journey, not near the beginning; and it is not given to me to know how many steps are necessary in order to reach my goal. Failure I may still encounter at the thousandth step, yet success hides behind the next bend in the road. Never will I know how close it lies unless I turn the corner. Always will I take another step. If that is of no avail, I will take another, and yet another. In truth, one step at a time is not too difficult. I will persist until I succeed.

What we need to understand is this: The monumentally great people of our lifetime, the tremendously successful achievers, have a better way of implementing the intense, burning desire about bigger dreams and goals than other people. That is the only difference. So, you can do whatever it is that consumes you, obsesses you, day and night. The saying comes to mind, "What the mind of man can conceive and believe, it can achieve with a positive mental attitude."

Do You Have an Intense Desire?

There are many people out there who will never, ever achieve anything monumental. They may never even achieve semi-monumental goals. They have wants and desires, but like many people, they will never develop the intense, burning desire needed to fan the flame and turn that want into an all-consuming desire. Why? It is simple: It is much easier to do nothing. Much easier to plod along day after day, working eight hours, getting paid mediocre wages, going home and doing whatever they want, enjoying their routine lives, and going back to the mundane job the next day, not really being happy with their jobs but never being truly motivated to the point of becoming consumed with changing their present circumstances.

There is nothing wrong with being average. Average people keep the country moving. Average is okay and completely acceptable in our society. But if you want to be different, if you want to change, then you must prepare yourself to make that commitment to achieve.

Entrepreneurial Spirit

I am amazed at how many young people are driven to succeed. I hear stories of how busboys working their way through high school work up the ladder of a restaurant business. They continue working in that restaurant after high school and through college. And that same busboy becomes a waiter, then a maitre d, and then ultimately the owner or partner in the same restaurant. That is true desire—the ability to keep your eye on the ball, never getting sidetracked, until the long-term goal is achieved.

> # We Are Each Born into This World Destined for Greatness!

Sam Walton was born in Oklahoma on March 29, 1918, on the family farm, where he worked until the family moved to Missouri. As a youth, Walton also worked at various odd jobs, including as a lifeguard, newspaper delivery boy, and waiter. He later worked at the JC Penney department store, and also served in the Army.

After the war, Walton opened up a variety store by scratching together money saved from his Army days and from his father-in-law. He was able to buy goods at super-low wholesale rates and to offer his goods for sale at very reasonable prices.

In 1962, Walton opened a five-and-dime store and eventually expanded across the country. By 1991, his retail enterprise was the largest in the world. Now Wal-Mart is world-renowned as the store with the great bargains, and his stores are thriving even in these economically challenging times.

I probably have traveled and walked into more variety stores than anybody in America. I am just trying to get ideas, any kind of ideas that will help our company. Most of us don't invent ideas. We take the best ideas from someone else.

—Sam Walton (1918-1992)

Chapter Seven

The Pros and Cons of It All

At times our own light goes out and is rekindled by a spark from another person. Each of us has cause to think with deep gratitude of those who have lighted the flame within us.

—**Albert Schweitzer** (1875-1965), Philosopher, theologian, physician

I had the pleasure of taking in a Mets and Nationals baseball game one Saturday in September. It was a thrill because I attended the game in the new Citi Field ballpark. I marveled at its brilliance in new brick, stone, and steel girders, the largest I had ever seen. The girders in the shape of a "Y" soared up a few stories, and, no doubt, supported most of the structure. I was fascinated by the great technology and workmanship that went into this great ballpark. So I looked up some statistics and learned that it includes 1.2 million bricks, 11,000 light fixtures, 2,200 doors, 850 televisions, 12,540 tons of structural steel and 48,000 cubic yards of asphalt. An amazing feat of construction, the stadium holds approximately 45,000 fans. I don't have statistics on how many people worked on it, but I can imagine fifty years from now some grandfather telling his grandchild all about how he helped build it half a century back.

I rarely go to baseball games, but when I do go, I get a real thrill out of watching the players on the field. I visualize what it was like for someone watching a game live in the 1920s or '30s. The players would have been stationed in basically the same spots as those who played this game. The uniforms would have been different, but the game was basically the same. The fans would clap and yell and stand and cheer. The players' dedication was basically the same—play hard and play your best because if you didn't, there would be someone sitting on the bench just waiting for that one opportunity to show the manager that he could play better than you and that he deserved to play full-time.

"Professional." The word itself has a nice ring to it. The Merriam-Webster Dictionary defines *professional* this way: "participating for gain or livelihood in an activity or field of endeavor often engaged in by amateurs."

Think of what it takes to be a professional baseball player and to play in Major League Baseball. The amazing thing is, a young boy with a baseball, a bat, and a glove can become the greatest baseball success ever. He needs an intense, burning desire that never fades. He needs so much more, but the fact remains that if the burning desire is not present throughout, he will never be propelled to greatness in the sport of baseball.

Every day is a new opportunity. You can build on yesterday's success or put its failures behind and start over again. That's the way life is with a new game every day, and that's the way baseball is.

—Bob Feller (1918-2011), Hall of Fame baseball player

When I think of the greatest baseball players of all time, I think of Lou Gehrig, Joe DiMaggio, Mickey Mantle, Hank Aaron, Babe Ruth, Cy Young, and many others. But the list is really not that long, considering that professional Major League Baseball has been played for more than one hundred thirty years—since 1876—by thousands of players over all those years.

To actually break into the Major Leagues is a very big accomplishment, considering that most of the people who put on a baseball uniform from childhood through adulthood will never actually make it that far. So, what is the difference between the players who make it and those who never make the cut?

Maybe it is only a 10 percent difference. Maybe one player is 10 percent faster than the others who never get called up. Ten percent? If a player has a batting average of 250, 10 percent better is 275. Or say one pitcher throws at eighty miles per hour and another pitcher throws at eighty-eight miles per hour. You see the small difference? That minute amount can mean a difference in pay of millions of dollars more once someone makes it to the majors.

So, I looked out onto the field while at the game, and I studied each player carefully as he manned his position. I watched the players in almost military precision as they guarded their ground, the area they were each responsible for, making sure there weren't any small mounds of dirt that would make a baseball take a bad hop if hit to them. I even studied the umpire as he bent down at the knees to look at every pitch. I looked closely as he studied each pitch of the ball so carefully. Then I realized that every pitch counts equally in value. One pitch could mean the ballgame for one team or the other. Some, if not most, pitches would be recorded in the record books. So it was no wonder how professional the umpire was. This particular umpire on this day was even crouching down behind the catcher when the pitcher was taking warm-up throws that didn't count for the game. I estimated that the umpire squatted down, bent at the knees, at least three hundred times for that game. Professional? You bet. Some umpires make it to the Major Leagues, too. Many, however, don't.

Professionalism is found in all walks of life. Think again about what it means to be "pro," and also consider those who merely go through the motions. I call some people "cons" because they are only conning themselves, making believe that they are giving it their best effort, while secretly, down deep, they are only trying to get to closing time.

> # We Are Each Born into This World Destined for Greatness!

William Henry "Bill" Gates III was born on October 28, 1955. Along with Paul Allen, he founded one of the most successful corporations of all time, the software company Microsoft.

In 1987, Gates was officially declared a billionaire in the pages of *Forbes'* 400 Richest People in America issue, just days before his thirty-second birthday. As the world's youngest self-made billionaire, he was worth $1.25 billion.

In June 2006, Gates announced that he would be transitioning from full-time to part-time work at Microsoft and to full-time work at the Bill & Melinda Gates Foundation. Their website states: "Guided by the belief that every life has equal value, the Bill & Melinda Gates Foundation works to help all people lead healthy, productive lives. In developing countries, it focuses on improving people's health and giving them the chance to lift themselves out of hunger and extreme poverty. In the United States, it seeks to ensure that all people—especially those with the fewest resources—have access to the opportunities they need to succeed in school and life."

The Gates Foundation now employees 858 people. They have established a trust account of $33 billion. Their total grant payments in 2009 were $3.0 billion. The foundation supports grantees in all fifty states and the District of Columbia. Internationally, they support work in more than one hundred countries.

Bill Gates and his wife are giving back to the world in which they have thrived. In an interview, Bill stated that he will give away 90 percent of his wealth. How many lives will be touched and changed by this one individual? How many will be so inspired that they will go on to become billionaires themselves?

Bill Gates once said, "Every day we're saying, 'How can we keep this customer happy? How can we get ahead in innovation by doing this, because if we don't, somebody else will.'"

Chapter Eight

Bad Things Happen to Winners, Too

Of course, very successful people have setbacks, too. It is not all a rosy road for them. Highly successful people find ways to get back up from the mat of defeat and claw their way back to the top of the ladder. It's as if they know in their hearts that they will be back on top again.

Let's look at some baseball superstars. Cy Young won 511 games as a pitcher. Most career hits ever: Pete Rose, 4,256. Most career stolen bases: Rickey Henderson, 1,406. Highest batting average: Ty Cobb, 366, which means out of every thousand at-bats, Ty Cobb got 366 hits and did it throughout his entire career. If anyone today can hit just three hundred out of every one thousand at-bats over his Major League career, he is guaranteed a spot in the immortal Hall of Fame in Cooperstown, New York.

One such great success, who met an untimely career end and, ultimately, death, was the great baseball hero Lou Gehrig. Lou came onto the scene in the Major Leagues in 1923 at the age of twenty. He spent the next sixteen years as a New York Yankee. Gehrig was given the nickname "The Iron Horse" because he would go on to play 2,130 consecutive games without sitting any of them out. This was some feat, especially in the days when a pitcher would pitch all nine innings, rest two or three days, and do it all over again. Players were tough back then—no babying any of them. He played a total of 2,164 Major League games.

Gehrig had seventeen seasons with the Yankees and would have kept going another five years or so. But something unheard of then happened to him. He became suddenly sick with Amyotrophic Lateral Sclerosis (ALS), what is now known as "Lou Gehrig's disease." No disease was supposed to attack "The Iron Horse," not at the strong and powerful age of thirty-six. But, yes, this amazing player suddenly couldn't play very well, and he couldn't understand why his hitting and fielding was sub-par.

This "iron horse" of a man, who had played 2,130 consecutive games, finally took himself out of the lineup. He broke his own consecutive streak, not realizing that he had a debilitating and ultimately crippling disease that would take his life approximately two years after his last game. Yet, in a farewell speech to his adoring fans at Yankee Stadium, he proclaimed himself the "luckiest man alive."

The luckiest man alive? Gehrig had an irreversible death sentence. But here is part of his speech:

For the past two weeks you have been reading about the bad break I got. Yet today I consider myself the luckiest man on the face of the earth. I have been in ballparks for seventeen years and have never received anything but kindness and encouragement from you fans.

So I close in saying that I might have been given a bad break, but I've got an awful lot to live for. Thank you.

Count Your Blessings

When I can't sleep, I count my blessings instead of sheep and fall asleep counting my blessings.

This line was taken from a very popular song sung by Bing Crosby in the movie *White Christmas*, which came out in 1954.

Count your blessings! We all know what that phrase means, but do we actually do it? The average person's life revolves so fast with so many things happening that I venture to guess most people do not truly count their blessings deeply enough.

It is said that we must chew our food carefully. Most people will contend that they, in fact, chew their food very carefully. But do they? The recommendation is to chew each bite thirty-two times. Now, I don't know who came up with the number *thirty-two*, but I can attest that I never chew thirty-two times! I usually chew barely enough to swallow. We don't really think much about it when eating because of everything else revolving around in our heads and lives at that moment. That is precisely my point: We take many things for granted—such as truly counting our blessings.

We are creatures of habit. For almost thirty years I have been getting my hair cut every few weeks by the same barber at the same location. I actually travel to another state now in order to visit my barber and receive my haircut. I feel a haircut is like a form of mental therapy, a healthy way to relieve stress. It is one of those actions that makes a person feel good about himself. We socialize with our hair professionals. We talk about what is on our minds, what is bothering us or them, and in the end we feel better about ourselves and life in general.

But on this particular day of my haircut therapy session, I got a rude awakening. It was around two o'clock on a workday. I had been in pain for most of the day, and it was a hectic day at that. The pain made the day seem longer and harder than it should have. So I abruptly got up, excused myself from my staff, and drove some ten miles away to get my hair cut. I almost always feel good after getting my hair cut, but this day I came away shocked and saddened.

Normally, my barber and I talk about some nonsense, some sports, or about our younger, wilder days. Sometimes we reminisce about some embarrassing things we did as much younger men, things we normally don't remember except at these special shared moments.

I realize that there is a special therapeutic mental escape that can be had in a mere haircutting session or, I would imagine, when a woman goes to a salon for her hairstyling or pedicure or facial. Maybe it has something to do with that short mental break we get by focusing on something other than our normal routine even for as few as ten minutes. It all helps the brain to redirect and take a momentary vacation—thus, a form of therapy.

But at this haircutting session, on this particular day, I felt like someone had suddenly hit me in my stomach with a sledgehammer. My barber, my friend of thirty years, disclosed to me that he had bladder cancer and nodules on his lungs. I sat in the barber chair in silent turmoil, trying to be my usual positive-uplifting-motivator self on the outside. I stayed optimistic on the outside as I listened to my friend explain how this latest hurdle in his life was very treatable.

But inside, I felt sad, and for days afterward I was in a state of shock. How could this healthy person in his fifties have such a terrible diagnosis? Then I thought, how can anyone get such bad news? Yet it happens every day and in every state in this country and in every country in the world. All too frequently, someone is diagnosed with a potentially life-threatening disease. They then must disclose this terrible news to their spouse, children, parents, friends, and coworkers.

Put yourself in the shoes of this newly diagnosed individual. Imagine what goes through his mind; how does one possibly deal with such potentially life-ending news? How does one cope, accept a diagnosis, get up in the morning and go out to work? How does one go on dealing with the unknown, the possibility of death? I thought about this for a long while. I thought about the sick people I had known well and how they portrayed their sickness and prognosis to all with whom they came in contact.

I came to this conclusion: Most of these sick and sometimes suffering individuals put on a good face for us, their family, friends, and coworkers. They try to minimize *our* pain, not theirs, by explaining how treatable their disease is. They may be right that their disease is quite treatable, and they should be as enthusiastic as they possibly can about their odds of beating the disease. But we, the healthy ones being told about this sudden prognosis, are naturally in doubt and full of compassion for the individual.

I believe that the suddenly sick and life-threatened persons we encounter are, in many cases, the bravest of all human beings. Many of them face sickness and death with a full-force approach and almost dare death to come near them. I draw strength from these fine individuals, many of whom we have lost to their diseases. Still, they bravely fought to the bitter end.

I believe God shows us these people for a special purpose—such notable people such as Patrick Swayze, Michael Landon, Christopher Reeve, and most recently Michael Douglas.

This is what reminds me every so often how precious and short our lives can be here on earth.

When it is all over, all said and done, what impact will my life have had on this world?

—JPC

Living Every Day of Your Life to the Fullest

One of the oldest people to run a marathon was Bhai-Faiya Singh, who, at age 94, ran the Toronto Waterfront Marathon in five hours, forty minutes, one second, setting a world record for the over-90 age group. Can you believe it? Ninety-four years old and running for almost six hours?

One of the oldest people in the United States passed away in September 11, 2009, at the age of 115 years and 148 days. Gertrude Baines was born in 1894. At age 115, Baines even voted in the 2008 presidential election, casting her ballot for Barack Obama "because," she stated, "he's for the colored."

My point is this: We know not how long we will grace this wonderful earth. We must anticipate becoming the "newest oldest" person on earth one day, but we must never ever put off our goals, the ones for which we will be remembered—not for one single day.

Famous by the Age of...

If someday they say of me that in my work I have contributed something to the welfare and happiness of my fellow man, I shall be satisfied.

—**George Westinghouse** (1846-1914),
American entrepreneur and engineer

I have always been intrigued by inventors. To me, an inventor possesses the great art of perseverance. They are great innovators, made up of something very special down deep inside. Failure is actually their stepping stone to victory.

In other words, a successful invention is expected, demanded even, by the inventor. The inventor in return commits himself to the task at hand, no matter how hard he must work, no matter how long it may take, and no matter how many failed attempts and experiments it may require. The only question in the mind of the great inventor is this: When will I have a successful working model?

It is a mindset, a tremendous positive mental attitude, that we each can adopt. In fact, I will go as far as to point out that each and every one of us in our own lives has used this great mental conditioning, this unending urge to succeed at whatever cost. We have each succeeded in something because we would not accept failure in that given endeavor. The only problem is that we forgot how to apply the same driving-force principles to other aspects of our lives as well.

Let me share some examples of how we perhaps have succeeded greatly. It could be something as small as studying for and passing an especially difficult course or a special test to acquire a license, perhaps to sell insurance or to operate certain types of specialized equipment or to manage buildings. I know I have; there have been times when I needed specialized licenses to sell certain forms of investments or insurance products. I remember programming my mind that "I will not fail. I will study in a certain manner and at a certain pace that will result in succeeding in the task at hand."

In these particular tests of endurance, perseverance, and will, the word *failure* was eliminated from my mind and replaced with a sign in my mind that flashed "SUCCESS!" When you program your mind with such a powerful command as "SUCCESS!" your mind will, in fact, find ways to help you succeed. Your mind may convince your body that it is really *not* that tired, or that you can and must study for one or two more hours, or that those negative thoughts will be drowned out by the positive thoughts that are being generated by the flashing "SUCCESS!" sign in your mind.

Believe and act as if it were impossible to fail.

—**Charles F. Kettering** 1876-1958, Inventor of the electric starter

You don't have to be brilliant to have brilliant ideas and outcomes.

At the age of nineteen, a Russian, Igor Sikorsky, almost had a working model of the first helicopter. By the age of forty-nine in 1940, Sikorsky's successful VS-300 became a model that others based theirs on, and Sikorsky was considered the father of the helicopter.

At the age of thirty-seven, Mary Anderson had the first patent for a windshield wiper. Her goal was to clean snow, rain, and dirt off car windshields years before Henry Ford's Model T automobiles were in production. On a visit to New York City in 1902, Anderson got the windshield-wiper idea while on a trolley car whose front window could not be kept closed because sleet made it impossible to see through it.

In 1829, at the age of thirty-seven, William Austin Burt invented the typographer, the predecessor to the typewriter. He worked at that time in the Michigan territorial legislature and later became a county Circuit Court Judge.

A fifteen-year-old grammar-school dropout from Maine invented an important and useful item. In 1873, while he was ice-skating with a new pair of skates, Chester Greenwood's ears were very cold. He went home and asked his grandmother to sew some fur onto wire shaped in the form of ears and attached to a metal band. Thus, the first set of earmuffs! The rest is history. Greenwood would ultimately establish a factory and produce earmuffs of a style still in use today.

Was Chester the most book-smart child of his day? No. But Chester was driven to greatness by dissatisfaction. He was dissatisfied by his present situation and was motivated to the action of changing it for the better. Initially, Chester probably had no intention of becoming an inventor whom the world would notice and recognize for something quite useful. Chester merely wanted to keep his ears from freezing. Many other people before 1873 had freezing ears, but they did not have the foresight and drive to work at the problem without stopping until they fixed it.

We each have the ability to excel. We can be great, and we can each be driven to fix a problem, right a wrong, or invent the seemingly impossible invention. Our mind can handle anything that is requested of it. But do we want something so badly that we will not stop until its completion? Will we be driven so intensely that we think about it endlessly?

Let's each learn to develop that powerful drive, that positive mental attitude needed to succeed. Do you want it badly enough? Because, you know, you *have* wanted *something* badly enough in your past that you refused to give in until you achieved success. It's all in the programming of that inner mind, that subconscious mind, that works magic whenever it is impressed strongly enough by the importance of a special goal.

Is There Gold at the Foot of the Rainbow?

I didn't know enough to quit. I was a dreamer who believed in the gold at the foot of the rainbow. I dared to go where wise ones feared to tread.

—King Camp Gillette (1855-1932), Inventor

The gold at the foot of the rainbow—what a great analogy. The great inventors and highly successful have the ability to focus on the gold at the foot of the rainbow. They have vision. They have fortitude. They keep their minds focused on the finish line, not on all the obstacles they encounter along the long, winding, and bumpy road to that finish line. The bumps and failures don't even faze the tremendously driven person. The failure is almost welcomed because the successful thinker knows in his heart that he will achieve success—it is only a matter of time. So, throw whatever distractions and obstacles you can at me, because I will prevail.

King Camp Gillette, a traveling salesman, was a perfect example of this mindset. He was born in Wisconsin in 1855, to a father who was a patent agent and to a mother who published a very successful cookbook called *White House Cookbook*. Frustrated at not achieving success, Gillette filed a few patents before getting advice from an employer who had his own ideas for inventing something disposable. Shortly thereafter, while shaving one morning before work, Gillette got very frustrated with his straight-edge razor that had become so dull it couldn't be sharpened.

It was then that Gillette got the idea for the disposable razor blade that could be replaced with a new sharp blade anytime it was needed. It took five long years to perfect his invention, using his own money. But, of course, he prevailed, and the disposable-blade idea is still in use today, though having been slightly modified over the years.

You see, there is usually some form of progression on the road to success. In Gillette's case, we see that his father owned his own business prior to becoming a patent agent. His mother was very successful in publishing a cookbook at a time when women usually did not excel so publicly. He went to work for someone who had just invented something very useful and who encouraged him to find something useful that could also be disposable. The seeds had been planted one by one over many years. Gillette's subconscious mind knew that he could be successful, mostly because others he knew had achieved success.

The man who found the historic sunken ship, the *Titanic*, is a perfect example of a person who thinks differently and is unfazed by all the negatives around him. It took Robert Ballard a full twelve years of off-and-on explorations—from 1973 until 1985—to locate the *Titanic* wreckage. Ballard said once, "All kids dream a marvelous image of what they want to do. But then society tells them they can't do it. I didn't listen. I wanted to live my dream."

Since its sinking on April 14, 1912, killing 1,517 people, the two-mile-deep *Titanic* had been sought unsuccessfully by many other explorers. But Ballard and his team realized that, like the sunken Navy submarines they were commissioned to find, the *Titanic* had imploded. The implosion and the great depths meant there would be literally thousands of pieces of debris scattered for miles at the bottom of the ocean. If Ballard could merely look for some of the debris field, he could then follow the debris to the ship itself. And on September 1, 1985, that is exactly what he and his team did.

Ballard thought outside the box. While others merely repeated other explorers' unsuccessful techniques, Ballard was steadfast in his beliefs and principles, and he succeeded where others failed. Ballard has also located other wrecks—the *Bismarck*, the *Lusitania*, the USS *Yorktown*, and John F. Kennedy's PT-109.

As to methods there may be a million and then some, but principles are few. The man who grasps principles can successfully select his own methods. The man who tries methods, ignoring principles, is sure to have trouble.

—Ralph Waldo Emerson (1803-1882),
American philosopher, essayist, poet

Chapter Nine

Success Is Within Your Reach

The more we read and absorb self-help books, listen to positive CDs, and search the Internet for inspirational stories, the more we convince ourselves that we, too, can be successful.

As a child watching variety television shows in the early 1960s, I observed all kinds of feats of excellence, from gymnastics to musical performances and more. I marveled at the various successful performers who made it to the "big leagues"—national television. But as I watched the acts, I slowly realized that I, too, could do the same act. I realized that I would have to practice a given task endlessly, but, yes, I, too, could excel and make it to television and perform.

Now, that is not to say that I can excel in every single field of performance, but if I worked very hard at any one task, I know I could become very proficient and might excel past others who were less committed than I. So my point is that if we continually search out success stories, study positive material, and limit how much we are exposed to negative influences, we can be convinced that we, too, can become successful.

Ben Cohen and Jerry Greenfield were childhood friends. After high school, Ben dropped out of several colleges and then took a job teaching pottery. Jerry attended and graduated from Oberlin College but was turned down for admission to medical school.

The two friends, unsuccessful up to that point, decided to open an ice cream store in Vermont. The first store was opened out of a run-down gas station. The friends began creating exciting and unique chunky ice cream flavors that quickly became favorites among their customers. By 1988, "Ben & Jerry's" stores were in eighteen states and thriving. By 2000, the Ben & Jerry's enterprise was sold to a company called Unilever for $326 million!

We measured our success not just by how much money we made, but by how much we contributed to the community. It was a two-part bottom line.

—Jerry Greenfield (b. 1951),
Co-founder of Ben & Jerry's Homemade Holdings, Inc.

We Are Each Born into This World Destined for Greatness!

Success is very subjective. We may each interpret what the definition of success is for our own lives. Success may mean a promotion, a new job, having a baby, or raising a family. Or to you it may mean becoming the CEO of a Fortune 500 company. You will slowly gravitate toward the level of what you most consistently desire in life. Carl Yastrzemski, the great baseball player, said, "I think about baseball when I wake up in the morning. I think about it all day, and I dream about it at night. The only time I don't think about it is when I'm playing it."

In Carl Yastrzemski's Hall of Fame acceptance speech of 1989, he said in part:

I can stand here—I can stand before you today and tell you honestly that every day I put that Red Sox uniform on I gave 100 percent of myself for my own. I treated it with dignity and respect in deference to our fans. A high regard for my teammates, coaches and management. Anything less would not have been worthy of me. Anything more would not have been possible.

Have you figured out what you truly want? Or are you just playing with time, as if you had all the time in the world to decide and to fight for what you will one day want? Goals. Dreams. Inspiration. Success never comes to people with mere *fleeting* dreams. Those who are truly successful are very driven individuals who never, ever stop thinking about and working at their dream or goal. Truly driven people sometimes can't sleep at night. They can't. Their brains are working furiously in overdrive, calculating, thinking, planning, and seeing their vision happen in their minds. Driven people are not followers; they are leaders marching to their own tune.

What the mind of man can conceive and believe, it can achieve.

—Napoleon Hill (1883-1970), American author

Vince Lombardi, the world-renowned football coach, said it best when he stated, "Winning is not a some-time thing; it's an all-time thing. You don't win once in a while, you don't do things right once in a while; you do them right all the time."

For a long time it had seemed to me that life was about to begin—real life. But there was always some obstacle in the way. Something to be got through first, some unfinished business, time still to be served, a debt to be paid. Then life would begin. At last it dawned on me that these obstacles were my life.

—Fr. Alfred D'Souza (d. 2004), Australian writer and philosopher

Chapter Ten

If We Only Knew What People Truly Thought of Us

He has achieved success who has lived well, laughed often and loved much; who has gained the respect of intelligent men and the love of little children; who has filled his niche and accomplished his task; who has left the world better than he found it, whether by an improved poppy, a perfect poem, or a rescued soul; who has never lacked appreciation of earth's beauty or failed to express it; who has always looked for the best in others and given them the best he had; whose life was an inspiration; whose memory a benediction.

—Bessie Stanley, Late 19th/early 20th century poet

How would you like to find out what the world really thinks of you, what other people like about you, and what they dislike, and what people feel you're doing right and wrong? How would you like to find out what changes you can make, in the eyes of others, to improve as a person, a leader, a business associate? The important question here is this: Can you really accept some constructive criticism? Many individuals want to change the world, but never believe that anything can or should be changed about themselves.

Imagine for a moment that you could get a complete analysis of the person you really are, or of your business. Whatever your situation may be—student, housewife, business owner, worker, and so on—I can show you how to get up to ten totally honest, straightforward opinions.

Yes, opinions of you and your personality, or of your business, and of how, in other people's opinions, you can improve many facets of your life, your business, and so forth.

Do you believe you can handle this type of constructive criticism? Would you actually look forward to seeing yourself through other people's eyes? And more importantly, would you be willing to make changes in your life or business practices to better yourself? Or do you feel satisfied in your own skin? Or nervous about what you might hear? Some people look forward to such feedback.

I've never met a person, I don't care what his condition, in whom I could not see possibilities. I don't care how much a man may consider himself a failure, I believe in him, for he can change the thing that is wrong in his life any time he is ready and prepared to do it. Whenever he develops the desire, he can take away from his life the thing that is defeating it. The capacity for reformation and change lies within.

—**Preston Bradley,** Early 20th century clergyman

How much would you pay for such an honest analysis? Is it worth a few hundred dollars to possibly change the rest of your life? Is it worth it to possibly improve yourself, any flaws you might have, and to reinforce through positive feedback the things you feel are your strongest traits or business practices? Tough questions. Tougher assignment.

Even the great Leonardo daVinci said, "I have offended God and mankind because my work didn't reach the quality it should have." So, don't ever be satisfied. Don't ever think, just because no one says anything to you, that you can't improve some areas of your personality, work ethics, marriage, business, friendships, and more.

Regardless of whether you own your own business or not, you can, in essence, secure from as many people as you want an honest evaluation of how they see you and your work. There is a special way you can receive a true and honest opinion. Here's how to do it:

First, buy some gift cards of whatever variety you prefer. They are sold online and are shipped to the recipients. You can purchase almost any denomination you feel comfortable with. Because I am in business for myself, and I feel that such feedback would be very beneficial, I would spend $50 to $100 on each gift card. You will send whichever gift card you choose to each person you would like to participate in your survey.

Next, and most important, depending on your particular situation, devise the questions that you wish to receive the all-important feedback on. As a business owner, and someone who relies upon independent salespeople to sell my products, I would set up my survey as follows and ask the following questions:

Sample Independent and Anonymous Survey

Listed below are some questions I would appreciate your answering as honestly as possible. Keep in mind that this is an anonymous survey and the purpose of it is to improve myself and my business. Only your totally honest answers will be useful. I have mailed out surveys to several different people in order to preserve your anonymity.

Questionnaire

Question 1:   In your opinion, what is John Carinci's best quality as a person?

Question 2:   In your opinion, what habit or trait do you believe could be modified to improve John Carinci as a person?

Question 3:   Looking at John Carinci, the businessperson, what improvement would you suggest?

Question 4:   What do you like about John Carinci's business, and why?

Question 5:   If you were the new owner of John Carinci's business tomorrow, what two main changes would you make, and why?

Any additional comments?

As you noticed in the survey, I stress that only honest answers will be useful to me. It's also important that you write a general letter and mail it with the survey to each person. Explain in the letter that it is a totally anonymous survey. Their answers will not be traced to them, and their honest responses will be appreciated. Also, explain that you chose them to participate in this survey only after careful consideration and that you will value the opinions you receive from all participants. Make sure to include the free gift cards. Explain in the letter that the gift is not in any way intended to buy their positive answers, but merely to pay them for their valuable time and effort in completing the survey.

Last but not least, go to the post office and buy #10 pre-stamped envelopes. Self-address the envelopes for the participants to use, and use your name and address as the return address. This way there will be no place on the envelope for the participant to place their name by mistake, and they won't have to address the envelope to you.

There is no doubt as to the usefulness of this questionnaire. You must send it only to the people you feel will give you their unbiased opinions, which you will need for optimum results.

The Man Who Dares

The man who decides what he wants to achieve
and works till his dreams all come true,

The man who will alter his course when he must
and bravely begin something new,

The man who's determined to make his world better,
who's willing to learn and to lead,

The man who keeps trying and doing his best
is the man who knows how to succeed.

—Author unknown

The Power of Observing and Learning

We can learn a tremendous amount by observing all that goes on around us. I've been motivated many times just by observing the people with whom I came in contact. I love to imagine myself practicing other people's careers. I try to picture myself for a while working at others' job duties, feeling their emotions, and thinking their thoughts. I do this not because I'm unhappy with myself, but rather to gain insight and inspiration in my own type of work.

Each time I go on vacation, I look closely at other people. I study them, their jobs, and their attitudes. I'll look at the hotel clerks and all other workers and wonder what it's like to do their work. What sense of gratification do they feel from helping others? How much satisfaction do they get out of their work, and are they happy, or do they just try to get to closing time and go home? I look at other people's work and wonder if it is fulfilling enough. Could I do it? How would I see myself and my attitude in five years' time if I were to do their jobs? I try to get inside their minds. Maybe it's the writer inside of me.

By looking around and observing, you can actually picture yourself doing some other line of work. You can look into other people's concerns and level of satisfaction without leaving your own job. I'm amazed when I think about all that actually goes on around us. There are days when, while driving to work, I look around and observe other drivers going to their destinations. And as I do, I think about our city, the state, the whole country. I think about the people working all sorts of different jobs: the police officers, firefighters, teachers, bakers, and so many others.

Even while we sleep, the cities, with all their nighttime workers, never do. Each night, all the major newspapers are cranking out their copies while most of us are snoring. This country runs like a well-oiled machine twenty-four hours a day. Even if you can't work for a while, our country keeps right on moving and churning.

It's amazing to me! I'm motivated by this positive work movement in our country. Even if you want to retire, you count on all the services around you to continue. This inspires me to do my part, to try to make my imprint, no matter how small it may be. It feels good knowing that I am helping to keep the country spinning.

We should all start to observe closely. It works best when you observe strangers. So, the next time you travel out of town, try using the observation technique. Look, listen, and feel. It doesn't cost you anything. But I guarantee that if you practice the technique, not only will you learn a great deal that you might have previously overlooked about the world around you, but you'll feel good about yourself. You'll also come away with a feeling of confidence and a new sense of ambition that will please and surprise you. Put yourself in that other person's shoes, even if just for a few minutes.

It feels great to be a contributing factor in the ongoing turning of the world. We all need to be reminded that we're not alone, that we each have to be a productive individual, and that we all need to rely on one another to do our best and help by pulling our own weight.

The people who get on in this world are the people who get up and look for the circumstances they want, and if they can't find them, make them.

—**George Bernard Shaw** (1856-1950), Playwright, political activist

Chapter Eleven

We Have the Ability to Change Someone's Life

Words have the power to destroy or heal. When words are true and kind, they can change the world.

—Buddha (Siddhārtha Gautama)
(ca. 6th century B.C.E.) Founder of Buddhism

How powerful are words? Can words, spoken or read, really change someone's life? Can words have a lasting effect, or are they lost in a split second?

It dawned on me one day that I could possibly change someone's life with mere words, either spoken or written. In fact, we all can! How powerful is that? With the pen I am holding at this moment and any scrap of paper I might write on, my words could have an immense effect on someone's life. Words that are read are a very powerful means of communication. My thoughts written down can translate into positive thought impulses in the mind of another person. These thought impulses can then propel that person forward into some sort of action, or change their present direction.

Handle them carefully, for words have more power than atom bombs.

—Pearl Strachan Hurd, Mid- to late 20th century poet

Words spoken have started wars, have initiated truces, have begun many a fight, and have been the cause of many murders. Words have broken up many relationships and have started other ones. Words. Mere words. A supreme example of the power of words is the Bible.

The Bible

The best gift God has given man is the Bible. It is by all odds the most influential book (or rather collection of books) in existence. The Old and New Testaments have held men together spiritually through the centuries. In 1611, fifty-four devoted English scholars and churchmen, assigned to the task by King James I, gave to the English-speaking world a monument of noble prose, on which so many of us have been brought up. The Bible has been translated into more than 1,150 languages. In short, the Bible has had the most dramatic career of any book in the world.

—Abraham Lincoln (1809-1865), 16th President of the United States

Words can inspire many a reader. Words also can motivate a writer to write thousands of words himself—perhaps even in just one sitting. I have been influenced by certain word-related subjects to the point that I could not stop writing, while at other times I had writer's-block. I have read the words of the greatest motivators, such as Og Mandino in his great self-help book, *The Greatest Salesman in the World*. And I have been motivated to great action for many years after reading W. Clement Stone and Napoleon Hill and their masterpiece self-help work, *Success through a Positive Mental Attitude*.

At a seminar in 1977, I met a great motivator and Olympic champion, Bob Richards. He was giving a motivational speech to all the agents of a life insurance company I had begun working for. I was only twenty-one and was struggling to make sales. After his speech, Richards took a few minutes to talk with me. He told me to go out and buy a copy of *Success through a Positive Mental Attitude*.

Well, the rest is history. I devoured that book, as well as other motivational books and tapes, and it changed my life forever.

Words spoken can change someone's life. Now, thirty-five years later, I am still in the life insurance business, I am running my own successful agency, and I am still practicing self-help techniques. So now I feel compelled to give back to society. I want to change the lives of young and old alike and to help people in foreign countries. I have had my first self-help book, *The Power of Being Different*, translated and published worldwide. There's no greater feeling than when someone tells you that the self-help book you wrote changed his life for the better.

We each have the power to motivate through the written word, the spoken word, and even mere acts of kindness. So try it out today. See if you can make someone's life better than before. Try to motivate someone to greatness. Make it one of your new goals. Watch how your enthusiasm becomes contagious.

I am a dreamer of words, of written words. I think I am reading; a word stops me. I leave the page. The syllables of the word begin to move around. Stressed accents begin to invert. The word abandons its meaning like an overload which is too heavy and prevents dreaming. Then words take on other meanings as if they had the right to be young.

—**Gaston Bachelard** (1884-1962), Poet, philosopher

Words That Live On and Touch the Soul

It was September 18, 2007, a normal Tuesday in the lives of many millions of people. But on this date a computer science professor, Randy Pausch, Ph.D., gave what is now known as "The Last Lecture." It actually *was* the professor's last lecture, given at Carnegie Mellon University. Randy Pausch, age 46, had been diagnosed with pancreatic cancer and was given only a few months to live. So why was he on stage in front of thousands of students and on video camera giving a speech? He was going to die. How could he get up and talk about life? Why? What was the purpose?

Mere words. Can mere words actually make a difference? To Randy Pausch, words were all he had to give back to the students who knew him so well, to his family that loved him, to his friends, and most importantly, to his three young children. Pausch wanted to leave a legacy, a blueprint for his children, aged 5, 2, and 1, to remember him by—a blueprint for them to use however they wished in their lives. But mostly he wanted everyone who ever knew him, and even the strangers who would come to know him, to know that death is "okay."

Pausch spoke about his childhood, about what he had learned all along the road to his success, and about wanting to thank people who had helped him along the way. His attitude was upbeat, not bitter. He was thankful for a full and challenging career. He appreciated life and all his successes. But what this dying man wanted to do more than anything was to give back. To help others. At a time when he could have been crying about his death sentence, or hiding in the comforts of his home, here he was, making people smile and teaching the life lessons he had learned in his forty-six years on earth.

Here are some of his words:

The brick walls are there for a reason. The brick walls are not there to keep us out. The brick walls are there to give us a chance to show how badly we want something. Because the brick walls are there to stop the people who don't want it badly enough. They're there to stop other people.

Don't complain. Just work harder. That's a picture of Jackie Robinson (the first black Major League Baseball player). It was in his contract not to complain, even when the fans spit on him.

Words can live on for centuries. Words can inspire someone for an entire lifetime. Words can also destroy someone for a lifetime. Therefore, be very careful what you say and how you say it. I guarantee that Pausch's last lecture will change many thousands of lives—far more, even, than he had hoped for. Pausch did succumb to the dreaded disease of cancer, but he made us all realize that this precious life we have all been blessed with is short and we must be brave, diligent, and aggressive in achieving our dreams and goals. Above all, we should be thankful for all that we do have.

Cherish your visions. Cherish your ideals. Cherish the music that stirs in your heart, the beauty that forms in your mind, the loveliness that drapes your purest thoughts, for out of them will grow all delightful conditions, all heavenly environment; of these, if you but remain true to them, your world will at last be built.

—**James Allen** (1864-1912), British author

A Man with Vision Changes the World

On December 7, 2009, Richard Branson unveiled SpaceShipTwo at Mojave Spaceport, California. SpaceShipTwo will carry people who purchase special tickets into space for the first time. Branson's company, Virgin Galactic, has been working on this unique vision for many years.

Only a man with real vision and dreams can carry out such an elaborate project of carrying everyday citizens into space for the first time. What kind of man could dream so big? Who is Richard Branson? Branson is a billionaire who has raised the funding himself. He has already booked over three hundred passengers at $200,000 each to fly in his space machines. He has collected over $42 million in ticket sales thus far.

Branson was born in 1950. At the age of sixteen, he was publishing a student magazine. In 1972, he began a recording label called Virgin Records. He sold the successful record company in 1992 for $1 billion. He started another record company in 1996 and has owned an airline, a credit card company, stores, a book publishing company, and more.

Branson loves doing the unheard of and has gone on to become very successful and respected in many industries.

For a successful entrepreneur it can mean extreme wealth. But with extreme wealth comes extreme responsibility. And the responsibility for me is to invest in creating new businesses, to create jobs, employ people, and to put money aside to tackle issues where we can make a difference.

—**Richard Branson** (b. 1950), British entrepreneur

Branson's spaceship will carry two pilots and six passengers. The ship will take off from a runway like a plane, but it will carry with it a rocket ship with rocket engines that will ignite at an altitude of fifty thousand feet and carry the ship into space. Branson plans his first space flight for the public sometime in 2011. It will be a dream that will have taken Branson at least eight years to realize and many millions of dollars spent trying to fly "regular" people into space. Will he be able to see his vision through to successful completion? I have no doubt.. And by the day of his first commercial flight to space, I imagine he will have in excess of one thousand passengers booked and paid for at $200,000 per person. Imagine the excitement on that day! It will be like the Wright brothers' first flight on December 17, 1903.

The Wright brothers accomplished the impossible, according to most people in 1903, when they flew the first powered airplane to a height of 852 feet. The rest is history. People with vision can change the world. The Wright brothers dramatically changed our world. They moved us ahead by maybe one hundred years with their airplane invention. Orville Wright said, "If we worked on the assumption that what is accepted as true really is true, then there would be little hope for advance."

He also said, "Isn't it astonishing that all these secrets have been preserved for so many years just so we could discover them!"

A man with a dream. It goes to show that the "impossible" can come to pass for a person with vision. Many of the inventions we take for granted today started with someone who said "Why not?" Who would ever think that we could speak on a wireless cell phone, then take a picture with the same contraption, hit a button, and send it across the globe in seconds to someone with another cell phone or a computer, and also be able to type out a message and send it via wireless to another person as far away as China—and all this in a split second!

So many of our dreams at first seem impossible; then they seem improbable; and then when we summon the will, they soon become inevitable.

—**Christopher Reeve** (1952-2004), Actor, director, producer

Inspired Determination

We can't all invent a space machine, or the wireless Internet that can be viewed on any cell phone anywhere in the world. But we can each dream big. We can think of the impossible, and we can, if we want something badly enough, bring it to pass. What is it that is deep within your heart and mind? What is your dream? Not a mere pipe dream, but something you lose sleep over. What is it that consumes your mind all the time?

I'll tell you my all-consuming desire. It is to finish writing this wonderful, enlightening, and motivating book. I get so pumped up with the various chapters and people I am writing about! I think about it during my day job of running an insurance agency. I think about it when I am trying to fall asleep at night. I am driven to write for hours every night, or while waiting in a doctor's or dentist's office. Even if I have only five minutes of waiting in some office, I write on scraps of paper.

This will be the seventh book I have written. But none before has been written with the speed with which I am writing this one. My hand can't write fast enough on the pad I am writing on. Am I driven, consumed? You bet! Do I have a vision about such a book? Yes! This is precisely what it takes to achieve a goal. We all have the ability to do something, but do we have the "inspired determination"? Are we willing to pay the price for success?

Success in book writing for me means three years minimum from start to finish. That is from the thinking stage to finished paperback. It can take as long as five to ten years to write a book. Talk about "inspired determination"! A book is a long journey for a writer. I contend that everyone has one great book inside just dying to be written. But will they be able to start and finish the long five-year marathon race needed to complete the task? I say most will not finish, and many will not even write the first word. Why? Maybe because it is not a burning and intense desire.

I remember buying my first acoustic guitar at age fifteen. As a lover of music, I decided that it would be great to play a folk guitar. Now, playing a musical instrument with any expertise is, in fact, a great accomplishment. I never learned to play that guitar, except for "Old MacDonald." My fingers hurt, I got discouraged, and the desire to play never persisted. It quite clearly was not an intense determination for me. That doesn't make me any less of a person. It just wasn't that important to *me*.

Well, guess what? Three months ago I got a brilliant idea. Yes, almost forty years later I wanted that folk guitar again, so I purchased one. I told myself that, no matter what, I wanted that guitar for what it represented to me.

So, why buy a guitar I may never play? I have a strange way of motivating myself. I can stare at this new, beautiful guitar and visualize great musicians playing their guitars. I visualize Johnny Cash, Neil Diamond, and even Elvis Presley. I visualize Harry Chapin, the great folk-style storyteller/singer/songwriter who died in a car accident. And it inspires me to do my *own* thing well.

You see, someone can take a cheap, old, used guitar, and all they have to do is work very hard. If they worked at it, they could master the instrument and one day go on to make a career for themselves. They could write one song, like Don McLean did when he wrote and sang "American Pie." Don McLean made a career out of that one hit song. Imagine that! You write one mega-hit song, and some thirty years later, the musician is doing shows and still selling albums of that very same song!

Yes, I draw inspiration from merely studying that guitar and what it represents. One of the least expensive hobbies in the world. I'm sure a used guitar could be purchased for twenty dollars on eBay. Some young person could be the next Neil Diamond—you never know. Then again, all the drive in the world does not make a rock star. There must be some natural talent to sing or write songs or play the instrument extremely well.

So, yes, I am inspired by that new guitar. It also brings back memories of many years ago. But my intense drive at the moment is elsewhere. Just maybe I might be inspired to write a new song simply by fooling around with that guitar when I am so inclined. But for the time being, I will be the rock star of self-help writers! I will make my own "music" with my pen and paper as I try to inspire one person each day.

You see, we all can be successful in anything we are consumed with. That doesn't mean we will make a million dollars at that one thing, but we will be good at it. I have heard many unknown guitarists who will never be famous playing the guitar with a great deal of expertise. But in their minds they are already a great success.

We Are Each Born into This World Destined for Greatness!

Amancio Ortega of Spain is, born March 28, 1936, is a Spanish fashion entrepeneur. He is Ranked by Forbes as Spain's richest man;

Europe's 2nd Richest man; and the 9th richest man in the World in 2010. He is personally worth $18.3 billion. He is now seventy-four and is a self-made billionaire.

Amancio was the son of a railway worker. He started a career as a "gofer" in a shirt store. He and his wife started making gowns and lingerie in their own living room.

Today, their business has over four thousand stores in seventy-one countries. Ortega is the chairman of the enterprise, and sales average $12.3 billion annually.

Chapter Twelve

The Long and Short of It All

Never put off until tomorrow what you can do today.

—Thomas Jefferson (1743-1826), 3rd President of the United States

I wondered about that Jefferson quote. So I did a little research. In 1900, the average man lived to a ripe old age of forty-seven. When Jefferson was in his prime, the average life span was maybe forty-two to forty-five years. No wonder there was a mad rush to accomplish goals in the 1800s.

Jefferson lost his wife of sixteen years when she was only thirty-nine. You see the mindset? So in those days, people were dying early. Sickness took the young and old alike. There were many deaths of young children. Today we have so many medical advances compared to in the 1800s. Yet, even for today, Jefferson was right: "Never put off until tomorrow what you can do today."

Today I received notification of the death of a business associate whom I have worked with for about twenty years. The man, David, was all of fifty-eight years old. He had been in perfect health until two months ago when he was diagnosed with an aggressive and rare cancer. In two short months he was gone. He had a good-paying and challenging job in insurance sales management. But the long and short of it all is this: We have no way of knowing what our longevity will be. All the money in the world means nothing.

Another associate I lost a few years ago had been the picture of health. John was around fifty years old. He had been married just a few years earlier at an older age than many marry. He had a child or two. John died suddenly from a very freak accident. His wife was driving on the highway with the children in the back seat and John in the front passenger seat. A truck driving in front of their car ran over a piece of metal that had fallen off the bottom of another truck. The metal catapulted from under the truck's tires through the family's front windshield and struck John in the neck. Only John was hurt, and he succumbed to his injuries less than a week later. Everyone who knew John was devastated. How could this healthy man be suddenly taken away?

Yes, medical technology is so advanced these days. There are so many lives saved each year, and the average age to which people live these days is growing by leaps and bounds. That still is no guarantee that anyone will live a long life. In my research for this book, I learned that during the Roman Empire, Romans had an approximate life expectancy of 22 to 25 years.

But here is the positive take on this subject, "the long of it": Average life expectancy has never been as long as it is today. Life expectancy today is over seventy-eight years. Life expectancy of an 85-year-old female, today, is age 92.

Best Time in the World's History to Be Alive

This is by far the best time ever to live your life.

We are going to be able, in a few years, to jump on a spaceship and travel into space. We all will be driving electric-powered vehicles very soon. We will have the ability to watch any show ever recorded, or movie ever shot, at a split-second recall right on our televisions. We will be able to ask for any program on our television via voice activation. Our computer will be reduced to watch-size and worn on our wrists. We will no doubt be able to prepare better meals in a fraction of the time it takes us now, freeing up more time for entertainment.

You see, there really is no better time to be alive than now. Medical procedures will become much more routine, less invasive, and more robot-precision-driven in technology. It is no secret that today's eighty-year-olds are as healthy as sixty-year-olds of twenty-five years ago. And many one-hundred-year-old people today are lucid for the most part. It is all quite unbelievable. But these are great times.

There are those who say there are too many dangers in the world and it was much better a hundred years ago. There is much doom and gloom in people's attitudes today. So let us look at history. History is the true indicator of times that have passed.

Just the Names and Dates Have Changed

Since the beginning of time, there have been thieves, murderers, and vicious people of all kinds, as well as wars. The term *terrorism* has existed for many centuries; its origin dates back to 1785. The definition of *terrorism*, in the Webster's Online Dictionary, is "the systematic use of violence as a means to intimidate or coerce societies or governments."

From the late 1500s to the early 1800s, the Barbary Pirates were a band of privateers who served as part of the naval forces of the Turkish Empire. The Barbary Pirates operated in teams from Tripoli and other parts of Africa. Their reign of terror lasted two hundred fifty years and became so fearsome that many nations, including the United States, for some time agreed to pay them an annual ransom just to ensure that their trading vessels could sail safely in the Mediterranean. The pirates used to capture vessels and enslave the personnel in those terror-filled years.

From 1860 to 1865, almost 620,000 Americans died in the Civil War, in which brothers killed brothers. Also known as the War Between the States, the Civil War's root causes were states' rights, slavery, and political and economic issues. If 620,000 people died, how many were wounded and crippled? What times they must have been!

In 1865, a man from Tennessee named Champ Ferguson was arrested, convicted, and hanged for the murders of more than one hundred people. He was one of the most feared men of his time.

In 1896, H. H. Holmes was convicted and killed for murdering as many as one hundred people. He was a feared and documented serial killer. Born in New Hampshire, he moved to Chicago, where he swindled people out of their money. After killing his victims, he either burned them or dissected them and sent their body parts to various places.

There will always be war somewhere. There will always be mass murderers, and there will always be terrorists in many forms and in many countries. Just the names and the dates will be different. There will be unrest in foreign countries, as there always has been.

We must not dwell on the doom and gloom that is so easily communicated throughout the world, but rather keep it all in perspective and go on with our lives. Allow others to dwell on the negative, end-of-the-world scenarios. Allow them to vent their anger and depression, but only allow a few seconds of those things to penetrate your mind. Limiting your exposure to bad news and negative influences allows you to maintain your drive.

The Will to Live and Prosper

I have always been inspired by the many stories of senior citizens who live long and prosperous lives or others who excel in many areas. One instance comes to mind: To date, nine men between ages 80 and 88 have run the New York City Marathon. Three women in their eighties have also run. All twelve finished the grueling 26.2-mile race. Thirty-two men aged 75 to 79 have run the race. The will to live. Yes, people today not only have the will to live, but they also have the will to stay in shape and take care of themselves. And with medical advances, we all are living healthier lives.

The oldest marathon runner in the world was ninety-eight years old. In September of 2009, he ran the Toronto Waterfront Marathon. As I am writing this paragraph about a 98-year-old marathoner, my knee is suddenly hurting. I admire the drive in many people. You see, we each have intense drives that propel us to the end of a chosen task or goal. What is urgent to you? What excites you so much that you can't get it out of your mind? Have you been inspired to action of any kind, after reading this book thus far? Have you now a newfound dream or goal? Take five minutes right now to formulate one new goal.

Some people can turn that intensely driven motor into gear whenever they wish. It's almost like the fine-tuned musician who can pick up a guitar and play a complete song after hearing it only one time.

I can psych myself up, almost at will, and turn that button on and rev that engine of "drive" all the way up. But it must be for a task that is near and dear to me. Recently, I found an old song which had been recorded in French by a pop artist fifty years ago. I was so moved by this unique tune that I couldn't get it out of my head. I am currently looking into how to acquire the rights to the song and have someone record it in English. But that is not all. I have asked many people to listen to the version I send them and to help me translate the words. But because I was having no luck finding a way to translate the lyrics, I decided to write my own original lyrics, and they came out great!

Even though I have written songs for forty years, I have never written words for another's melody, much less a French tune. So you see, we can do anything we are highly motivated to do. But you must want it badly. You must turn that special switch on, that intensely driven switch, the one that, once turned on, cannot be turned off until the goal has been reached. That switch was also turned on for me as I wrote the first word of this book, and it won't be turned off again until the first copy of the paperback comes off the presses. So that brings us to highly driven people who lead full, active lives and somehow manage to outlive many other people. Is it a fluke? Is it luck? Or is it something in their minds that doesn't allow sickness to infiltrate their bodies?

Can Thoughts Prolong Life?

Something to live for. Something to hope for. The refusal to die. The refusal to allow negative thoughts to penetrate their minds. The refusal to contemplate their own age. Is it possible that some people can will themselves to live longer, while others knowingly or unknowingly will themselves to die prematurely? I believe most certainly that people do will themselves to live a long, healthy life or will themselves to die.

Just to give you an example of longevity in our world today: Recently on the world news there was a story of a woman, aged 100, who was killed by another woman, aged 98, who had dementia. Both were residents of a nursing home. Strange? Yes. Maybe even some new kind of age record for victim and killer. But in any event, many people are living very long lives. Granted, some are sharp of mind, and many are not sharp. I venture to guess that in the future we will be extending ages of the elderly to 120, and their minds will be sharper than eighty-year-old minds of today.

But I want to bring to light older people who have made their marks in the past. We may in fact be able to live a long and healthy life. In fact the odds are that we will. The question I have for you is this: Will you be content with the results you have compiled in your long life on earth?

Our deepest fear is not that we are inadequate. Our deepest fear is that we are powerful beyond measure. It is our light, not our darkness that most frightens us. We ask ourselves, who am I to be brilliant, gorgeous, talented, fabulous? Actually, who are you not to be? You are a child of God. Your playing small does not serve the world. There is nothing enlightened about shrinking so that other people won't feel insecure around you. We are all meant to shine, as children do. We were born to make manifest the glory of God that is within us. It is not just in some of us; it is in everyone. And as we let our own light shine, we unconsciously give other people permission to do the same. As we are liberated from our own fear, our presence automatically liberates others.

—**Marianne Williamson** (b. 1952), Spiritual activist and author

The oldest practicing lawyer in Massachusetts was a man named Reuben Landau. Reuben was practicing law every day with his son Bill. At age 103, Reuben refused to retire. He worked until he became ill, three weeks before he passed away. The elder Landau was sharp right until he passed on.

Maybe working every day kept him young. Maybe his refusal to rust away like some old car from 1904 kept him alive. Imagine that—a car from the year of Reuben Landau's birth would have to be from 1904! That puts into perspective how old he was in 2007. Age really is a state of mind. Attitude is so important. The attitude of "Why not?!" is so important. The question may come up, "Are you sure you want to continue working at your age?" And the answer that comes from the heart and mind of the centenarian is, "Why not?!"

You see, they know in their minds that they are over 100, but they immediately discount it, staying sharp, staying current with the times, and growing rather than dwindling away.

Life is not a journey to the grave with the intention of arriving safely in a pretty and well-preserved body, but rather to skid broadside, thoroughly used up, totally worn out, and loudly proclaiming: WOW, what a ride!

—**Author unknown**

Edna Parker was born in 1893 and died in 2008. She lived to the ripe old age of 115 years and 220 days. For some time Edna was considered the oldest person in the world. She attended college, became a teacher, lived on a farm, had two sons. She loved to read; she enjoyed poetry and recited poetry to her visitors.

As of September 2009, there were twenty-three people who were validated to have lived to the age of 115. Amazing! There are certain genes that contribute to longevity, no doubt. But there are also thought patterns that, I believe, shave many a year off someone's life. Imagine if we could only perfect the "special formula"!

To live to age 115, someone would have to live over 42,000 days. Amazing! Can you imagine that? The number of people over age 100 in the U.S. today is more than 84,000. By the year 2040 it is estimated that number will grow to 580,000. My suggestion: Watch what you allow to seep into that computer-mind that so skillfully runs the manufacturing plant we call our bodies.

Sarah Knauss lived to be 119 years and 97 days old. She lived her entire life in Pennsylvania. She was a homemaker, worked in an insurance office, and was healthy most of her life. Her daughter explained her mother's longevity this way: "She's a very tranquil person, and nothing fazes her. That's why she's living this long." Her daughter lived to the age of 101 herself.

What Will We Be Remembered For?

Life is no brief candle for me. It is a sort of splendid torch which I have got hold of for the moment, and I want to make it burn as brightly as possible before handing it on to future generations.

—**George Bernard Shaw** (1856-1950), Playwright, political activist

There is a story of one man who suddenly worried what his obituary would say about his life after he passed away.

One day, Alfred B. Nobel's brother passed away, but a newspaper inadvertently ran the obituary all about Alfred, the surviving brother. Alfred was horrified after reading what his own obituary would say about him if he died that very day. You see, Alfred B. Nobel was a well-known Swedish munitions manufacturer, known as a man who invented the means to kill more people with his dynamite explosives than anyone else in history had done. Nobel made up his mind at that moment to change how he would one day be remembered.

Alfred B. Nobel did change how the world would remember him, by creating the world's most famous set of awards, known as the Nobel Prizes. Since 1901, the Nobel awards have been presented yearly for outstanding achievements in literature, peace, economics, medicine, and the sciences. When Alfred Nobel died, he left behind a fund and specific instructions in his will as to how to carry on with the prizes each year. What a legacy! In 2009, President Barack H. Obama was awarded the Nobel Prize for Peace.

While writing this section, I thought about how my obituary would possibly read, and honestly I was not satisfied. What a wake-up call. I have so much more to accomplish. It's great to be shocked back to reality every so often.

When you remember me, it means that you have carried something of who I am with you, that I have left some mark of who I am on who you are. It means that you can summon me back to your mind even though countless years and miles may stand between us. It means that if we meet again, you will know me. It means that even after I die, you can still see my face and hear my voice and speak to me in your heart.

For as long as you remember me, I am never entirely lost. When I'm feeling most ghost-like, it is your remembering me that helps remind me that I actually exist. When I'm feeling sad, it's my consolation. When I'm feeling happy, it's part of why I feel that way.

—**Frederick Buechner** (b. 1926), Writer and theologian

I am contemplating this quote of Buechner on remembering. It is scary to think of one's own passing. We quickly push it out of our minds. I know it pushes me on. It jolts me forward like an electrical shock. The question "What will I be remembered for?" is a troubling question. But for me, I believe with all my heart and soul that after life on earth, we each get to graduate to the next level—the hereafter.

I believe that in the hereafter we are very much aware of every second we spent on earth, and we get to dissect each second of life spent here in great detail. Imagine that. Imagine knowing all the good, the bad, the ugly of all our actions. Imagine knowing each good deed or bad deed, and everyone we ever touched positively, and whom they, in turn, were able to touch.

This actually motivates me to make a difference today. Right now, not putting off anything to tomorrow. One thing I am guaranteed is *Now*. Right now is ours—we own our today—because we have been blessed for this one day. Did you work toward your goal with the one day you own—today? Or was it mostly a wasted day? Motivate yourself to think like the great man Alfred Nobel, who vowed to change the way the world would remember him. We don't have to be famous or wealthy to be fondly remembered. We just have to touch many people who, in turn, will touch many. And in the end, your one act can inspire, indirectly, many millions. Remember: whoever you are, rich or poor, at the top of your field or not, employed or out of work, *you are the greatest miracle in the world!* Don't ever forget that.

One Act of Kindness

A story about an act of kindness circulates on the Internet. The author is unknown:

Paid For by a Glass of Milk

One day, a poor boy who was selling goods from door to door to pay his way through school found he had only one thin dime left, and he was hungry.

He decided he would ask for a meal at the next house. However, he lost his nerve when a lovely young woman opened the door. Instead of a meal, he asked for a drink of water.

She thought he looked hungry so she brought him a large glass of milk. He drank it so slowly, and then asked, "How much do I owe you?"

"You don't owe me anything," she said. "Mother has taught us never to accept pay for a kindness." He said, "Then I thank you from my heart."

As Howard Kelly left that house, he not only felt stronger physically, but his faith in God and man was strong also. He had been ready to give up and quit.

Many years later, that same young woman became critically ill. The local doctors were baffled. They finally sent her to the big city, where they called in specialists to study her rare disease.

Dr. Howard Kelly was called in for the consultation. When he heard the name of the town she came from, a strange light filled his eyes.

Immediately, he rose and went down the hall of the hospital to her room. Dressed in his doctor's gown, he went in to see her. He recognized her at once.

He went back to the consultation room determined to do his best to save her life. From that day he gave special attention to her case. After a long struggle, the battle was won.

Dr. Kelly requested the business office to pass the final bill to him for approval. He looked at it, then wrote something on the edge and the bill was sent to her room.

She feared to open it, for she was sure it would take the rest of her life to pay for it all. Finally she looked, and something caught her attention on the side of the bill. She read these words:

"Paid in full with one glass of milk.

(Signed) Dr. Howard Kelly."

Tears of joy flooded her eyes as she prayed happily, "Thank You, God, that Your love has spread abroad through human hearts and hands."

Every so often we get a wake-up call to put our goals and dreams on the front burners and move in the direction that will see the tasks to fruition. I feel that I am in fairly good health, though I have the normal aches and pains of a middle-aged man. But the other night I was given a rude awakening.

I was trying to adjust a timer we set up to control our exterior Christmas lights. It was dark, so I went out onto my rear yard deck through my home's sliding patio door. As I walked onto the deck and closed the patio door behind me, the door suddenly locked me outside. So, after I had adjusted the timer, I proceeded to walk down the wooden patio stairs, and I slipped. My feet went up in the air, and I landed very hard on my back, right on the wooden stairs. Everything hurt but nothing was broken. I learned that the wooden steps had ice on them even though there was no ice elsewhere.

Over one week later, everything hurt: my back, my hands that broke some of the fall, and some pulled muscles. But what really hit me hard was this: If I had hit my head really hard, I could have been killed or paralyzed. Life is just that precious. Someone who is in perfect health could have an unfortunate accident that ends his life.

Just today I learned that an insurance friend of mine skidded on a patch of black ice and hit a guardrail. His car flipped over and landed on its roof. My friend was smart enough to have worn his seat belt and got away with some minor injuries. Talk about a wake-up call that makes you put everything in perspective. After a sudden wake-up call like that, petty things just don't bother you anymore, and you look at life with a new set of eyes, thanking God for all the good you still have.

Maybe it is my age, but I feel like I hear more hard-luck stories of late. It is important to put these sometimes-sad stories into perspective. I try not to dwell on sad stories for too long. But I also believe that there is a fine line between not dwelling on sadness, and ignoring it completely. I feel we must extract a lesson from each story. We must learn from another's sadness and then store the sadness away in a file deep within the recesses of our minds, retrieved later only to remind us of the lesson the story carries within itself.

Just today I met with a marketing director who works for a prominent insurance agency that I decided to give some of our agency's new business to. The rep told me of how he became disabled and deeply in debt due to a bad car accident he had been in over three years earlier. The person who was driving the other vehicle rear-ended this man. But the person who caused the accident had no car insurance and no assets.

My contact had to stop working for almost a year, leaving him with no income and in terrible pain. Now, over three years later, he is able to work again but still suffers ramifications and pain from that accident.

The lesson I took away from the gentleman was this: Not everything that seems pressing and urgent in business each day is worth getting upset over. And there are more important things in life, like his small child, his wife, his family.

Once again—put it all in perspective.

A Little Encouragement Goes a Long Way

Sometimes a small word of encouragement can go a great distance in motivating one onward to new and lofty goals. Today an old acquaintance called me from far away. We hadn't seen each other in almost twenty-five years. He called me to tell me that he was reading one of the books I had written. Since he had never read one of my books before, I was interested in his assessment.

When he told me that he had been reading my book until four o'clock in the morning and he couldn't put it down, it made me feel great—not because I wanted to hear someone else tell me that my writing was riveting, but because I wanted to hear that someone whose opinion I respected a great deal was actually enjoying one of my books.

I thought about the impact that a well-placed kind word has on a person. As a writer, where it takes anywhere from three to five years to completely write a new book, it is very encouraging to receive positive feedback. In fact, just one honest and very positive statement from another can actually motivate me to complete a new project. In my case, the positive feedback helps push me to drive forward with my next book. And when a book can take up to five years to complete, with many hurdles along the way, it is those well-placed comments that I remember so well. I draw on the positives from my past writing successes to help with whatever current writing difficulties I am facing. So the next time you think a positive thought about someone, don't hesitate to let him or her know it. Maybe that comment will stay with them for many months to come.

> ## We Are Each Born into This
> ## World Destined for Greatness!

In 1977, Mrs. Debbi Fields, at age 20, with no business experience, opened her first cookie store. Debbi persuaded banks to finance "Mrs. Fields Chocolate Chippery." The rest is chocolate-chip history. Mrs. Fields Cookies are enjoyed by millions of people all over the world. In the 1990s the company was sold to an investment firm. Mrs. Fields and her husband became very wealthy with a simple concept: great chocolate chip cookies!

Chapter Thirteen

Pack as Much as You Can into Life

Enjoy the little things in life, for one day you may look back and realize they were big things.

—Robert Brault

I love to study people—all kinds of people, from all walks of life. I study young children who are all-loving, who know not of prejudices and hatred yet at their young ages. I study their eyes, dancing with life and love. Children can teach us so much. Thank God for young children. It is unfortunate, though, that some adults, unaware of the long-term ramifications, feed destructive thoughts into young children's computer-minds, influencing them negatively as they mature.

I study adults, too, specifically seniors who have experienced many years of life. I study their outlooks on life, their past, and the future. I try to understand their acceptance of a life that may soon end. I wonder what goes through their minds with regard to their ultimate passing, and I marvel at how accepting some are about the fact that their time on earth is coming to an end. I observe in many seniors a calm acceptance of the inevitability of their life one day coming to an end. Is it that they have had their fill? Are they tired? Have they felt they have accomplished enough? And are they satisfied? I watch. I wonder. And I study closely all manners of people.

We learn by careful observation. We can each improve our lives if we only try not to fall into the mistakes made by those we observe closely. After all, aren't we always trying to reinvent ourselves, improving and changing, hopefully for the better?

Many seniors tell me, "If I am alive next year . . ." or "I probably won't be here next year." This used to bother me, until I realized that they are realists; many seniors their age may, in fact, not be here in one year.

I also wonder if, in fact, a person's body will actually comply with their inner thoughts and simply shut the human manufacturing plant down. In other words, if a person is really, truly tired and has little to look forward to, and their drive to survive has diminished, does that person's body "rush" to shut down? And on the other hand, does a person's drive to continue onward with life's journey on earth keep them alive just a little longer?

All this has come to mind recently in light of what I have busying myself with of late.

What Will You Be Remembered For?

I am doing a great deal of research for what will become my eighth book. This new endeavor came about by sheer accident. Lately, I like a good challenge when writing a new book. Maybe I like to write outside my comfort zone every so often. Well, this is what is currently challenging me. I actually put the book I *was* writing on hold for the sake of the new, more challenging one.

It all started quite innocently while surfing eBay for what I call treasure gems, be they autographs, old magazines, historical finds, or whatever. Well, this particular time, I came across a diary from 1923 in Hagerstown, Maryland. I was intrigued by the year, and by the fact that a girl or woman had written the diary, which covered the entire year of

1923. Almost three hundred sixty pages were written out by hand in pencil, and fairly neatly, too.

Well, I won the auction for the diary, and as I began reading all about this unknown girl and became more intrigued, I decided to base a novel loosely on her and her times, revolving around a good mystery, of course.

What really caught my eye while reading the diary was how many of her family members passed away or became sick, and how many times she herself was very sick, during that year. Her father and a few relatives died between the ages of 46 and 68. I researched some children of that period who died at age ten or younger.

When I tried to research her last name, "Bloom," to find out her true identity, I realized that many people are forgotten far too quickly after their passing. It took four hundred hours of research to find the dairy writer's first name; the fact that she was twenty-one at the time; the names of her father, mother, brother, husband, and son. I was able to secure obituaries for all of them except her. I became consumed with finding out who this woman had been and who she became later in life, as her words in the diary intrigued me.

What I took away from my research was this:

- Every day should be lived as if it is your last on earth.
- Family and friends should be ultra-important in your life and should be seen regularly.
- We should reflect often on our lives and thank God every day for all the blessings we have.
- And last, we should strive to improve the state of humankind, if only in some small way, and look to be remembered for many years after we pass on.

In 1923, there were no televisions—only radios and Victrolas. Movies at a theater were a huge treat. Dancing was very big and enjoyable for this twenty-one-year-old and her friends. Much enjoyment was derived from canoeing, taking a ride in a 1920 Ford that would often break down, and sitting with a boyfriend on a two-seated swing in the yard.

Miss Bloom's days were filled with visiting and entertaining many relatives and friends, and cooking and baking pies and cakes for them was routine. You see, Miss Bloom led a very busy life in those days, as I realized that many people in that time period did. Life was so very unpredictable in 1923, that it was as if they were chasing after as much as possible before it could slip away.

At times our own light goes out and is rekindled by a spark from another person. Each of us has cause to think with deep gratitude of those who have lighted the flame within us.

—Albert Schweitzer (1875-1965), Theologian and physician

There is a great lesson in this story. It shows how fortunate we are to be alive in the current period of time. You see, when Miss Bloom got sick, as she did several times that year, the doctor had to make many house calls over the course of the ten days it took her to recuperate. Routine sicknesses that don't set us back at all today robbed many of their lives in those days. I was happy to see that Miss Bloom did live to get married in her early twenties and had a son and a grandson, who were very prominent attorneys and who, in turn, made huge impacts on the world around them.

Miss Bloom quotes a great poet, James Russell Lowell: "Be noble, and the nobleness in others will rise in majesty to meet thine own." And she intrigued me further with another quote: "Boast not thyself of tomorrow, for thou knowest not what a day may bring forth."

My message echoes hers: Pack as much as you can into this life with which you have been blessed!

My Aggressiveness Will Lead to Opportunities for My Success

For as long as I can remember, I have been considered a go-getter. I am aggressive in all that I undertake. I don't know exactly how I came to the decision to be so aggressive in my actions. Perhaps I realized early on that being so aggressive and consciously trying to be different than most others around me would give me an edge. Maybe it was an assumption I had, as a child, that others were superior to me in many ways. I am not sure exactly why, but my wanting to do more by being so aggressive has stuck with me all these years. And my advice to this day is: Always do more; be more aggressive in your actions and duties than the next person. But more important, try always to be different from those all around you. With this special mindset, you will ultimately excel in life and business.

At the time of this writing in 2010, there still are opportunities galore available to all who truly want to succeed at something special. If the opportunity is not down one road, it may lie down a different road not far out of reach. But one thing remains as constant as it has been for thousands of years: Those who will work long, hard, and smart in all their activities will usually succeed. And then again, those who are lazy in their thinking and striving, and who are complacent in action, will usually lag behind those who greatly succeed.

Perfect examples of success in today's world are those young and ambitious people who work the Internet to their advantage. They may invent a new website or gadget that is cutting-edge in saving people money or simplifying people's lives in some unique and inventive way. Look at the new Apple iPad, which has become an instant success. It really is amazing and only goes to prove that the future of computing will be mind-blowing. We cannot even comprehend the advancements that will come along in the very near future.

We will, no doubt, one day be able to bring forth images on a screen by merely thinking certain thoughts in our minds. The technology we all thrive on is moving very fast. Keep in mind that imagination and hard work are ingredients that present-day entrepreneurs use to separate themselves from others on the playing field of life. Sometimes the payoff for some of these imaginative entrepreneurs is in the form of many millions of dollars.

One such present-day success story seems quite simple. It started innocently enough with the high school art project of a young woman named Lindsay Phillips. She came up with the inventive idea of adorning the tops of shoes with buttons and ribbons. She further expanded her project to incorporate Velcro to hold the ribbons onto the straps of flip-flop shoes. And with that unique and brilliant idea, a new company was formed.

A few short years later, Lindsay Phillips now heads up a company with sales in the $18 million range. Her unique "SwitchFlops" are now carried in over three thousand stores. And her "SwitchFlops" now feature over eighty interchangeable straps, all utilizing the Velcro technology to allow the consumer to mix and match the flip-flop shoes to the outfit worn for the day.

Is Lindsay brilliant, lucky, inventive, hungry, driven, or just imaginative? Here, clearly, was a young woman with a vision. It goes to show that if one is consumed with desire and opportunity, they, too, can excel.

We Are Each Born into This World Destined for Greatness!

Born in 1910, Mother Teresa was a truly great human being who excelled during our lifetime by dedicating her life to helping those in great poverty and need.

Born in Albania as Agnes Gonxha Bojaxhiu, she took her vows in 1937, and taught at Saint Mary's High School in Calcutta for almost twenty years.

Mother Teresa felt moved to help the poverty-stricken people of India and established the Missionaries of Charity, which was later expanded into many chapters across the globe. In 1950, she began a care center for patients of leprosy. Mother Teresa was awarded the Nobel Peace Prize in 1979 and accepted it on behalf of the "poorest of the poor." She passed on in 1997. She once said, "I see God in every human being. When I wash the leper's wounds, I feel I am nursing the Lord himself. Is it not a beautiful experience?"

Chapter Fourteen

The Never-Ending Will to Succeed

Do the one thing you think you cannot do. Fail at it. Try again. Do better the second time. The only people who never tumble are those who never mount the high wire. This is your moment. Own it.

—**Oprah Winfrey** (b. 1954), Talk-show host, philanthropist

It is no big secret that those who succeed greatly have that never-ending, burning desire. Deep in their hearts they have a dream, something big and grand, something they want more than anything in the world. Maybe it's a little girl with a big singing voice who wants to become a famous singer. Maybe it is a young man named Clinton, who was so impressed after meeting President John F. Kennedy that he was inspired and intensely motivated to one day become the president of the United States himself.

Recently I saw a video of President Obama visiting a classroom of very small children. It might have been a kindergarten class. All or most were of African-American descent. The president was going to read a book to them and share a basket of cookies with the class. All I could think about as I saw the sixty-second sound byte was this: How many of these young and very impressionable children will be positively inspired for their lifetime as a result of this experience? How many of these children will go on to college and earn a degree? Inspiration and motivation can last forever. I believe that, on average, more of these children will be successful in their lives than a class of kids of similar economic status and race somewhere else who did not meet the president.

One smile, one handshake, one cookie handed to a child can change his life. Mindset? Inspiration? Subconscious programming? Whatever the reason, these children will be changed for life. Inspiration is enormous in value. How many great, successful individuals were moved in such a way when they were younger? Maybe it was a teacher, a priest, a nun. Maybe it was a father, a mother, or even an actor or a singer. The mind is such a powerful computer that it will find a way to bring about that which is so intensely desired as a result of such inspiration.

The Dream That Just Won't Die

Is there a special dream deep inside you that just won't die out? A flame that burns inside your mind and heart? Truly successful people talk about such a dream and desire that has propelled them to greatness. Success very rarely happens by mistake and never without hard work. There is story after story of how a person worked endlessly toward that goal and dream.

Tiger Woods is a perfect example of someone who just fell in love with the game of golf at a very early age. He tells how he appeared on the Mike Douglas television show demonstrating how well he could play golf at the age of perhaps three.

He also tells how well his father played and how this spurred him on to excel in the sport. And even when he was a baby, his mother could get a spoonful of food into his mouth only when he turned to watch his father practice his golf game. In short, Tiger's father was the motivating force that encouraged Tiger to want to be a great golfer. And he is the greatest who ever played the game.

By age 33, Tiger had already won ninety-three golf tournaments, including four Masters tournaments, and was awarded "Athlete of the

Decade" by the Associated Press. Tiger Woods has earned in excess of $1 billion from his golfing and endorsement efforts. No other athlete has earned as much as he has in the history of sports.

I always feel pressure. If you don't feel nervous, that means you don't care about how you play. I care about how I perform. I've always said the day I'm not nervous playing is the day I quit.

—**Tiger Woods** (b. 1975), American professional golfer

The media is all abuzz about Tiger Woods these days. His personal life and marriage have unraveled because of his careless lifestyle. But no one can ever take away his extraordinary accomplishments in the area of sports.

I do wonder, though, about some extremely successful people—how, after working for so many years to reach monumental accomplishments, some seem to self-destruct. I believe that some of these people can't handle their success. Maybe it's because we idolize the extremely successful so much, putting them high up on a pedestal, giving them no privacy. It seems we follow their every movement and breath. Maybe some of these very successful people, who were one day like you and me, cannot accept the intense level of fame they have achieved.

Principles of Success

Separate yourself from the crowd by remembering and following these success principles:

1. Formulate Powerful and Challenging Goals:
    We need to challenge ourselves to think and act outside the box, so invest the time and effort to set specific and challenging goals. These goals should be attainable, yet ones that make you stretch, make you test yourself, to a point that you wonder if you will be able to achieve them. Most people will not attempt

to set such goals because they don't want to be challenged by the long road of work it takes to achieve them.

Writing a new book is the type of goal that will test the inner strength and determination of the average person. Because of the time it takes to finish such a project, it challenges the average person.

2. Be Consumed with the Achievement of Such a Goal:

As with any worthwhile and rewarding accomplishment, one should be consumed with the achievement of such a goal. *Consumed* means that the goal is ever-present on one's mind; the achievement of the special goal is planted deep within the subconscious mind. The goal should be a true yearning, a burning desire felt continuously throughout one's day, encouraging one toward its completion. As with the greatest inventors, who are consumed with completing a successful invention, your goal should become that positive mental splinter that keeps sending signals that this goal must be completed.

3. The Point of No Return:

Once committed, the mind cannot be allowed to back out of the achievement of such a goal. Let's assume that the major undertaking is the building of a patio deck at your home. A trick of committing yourself to its ultimate completion is the announcement of the project to all around you. In other words, take pictures of what the deck would look like, and post them all over the workplace and home living area. Now, when someone asks you about it, explain, "That is the deck I am going to build." Make sure there is a date on the picture and a mark on the calendar showing clearly the intended completion date. This trick will enforce your commitment to the achievement of this task.

4. Reward System for Goal Achievement:

All worthy goals that have been achieved after long, hard work must be rewarded. It is important to have what I call "Happy

Celebrations." Let's say I undertake the tremendous goal of writing a book, and it takes a full three years to complete. I can attest that such an undertaking is quite difficult and requires a special dedication. The reward could be a short vacation, a special Broadway show, and dinner, or the purchase of some kind of a gift desired for some time. The reward system reinforces the Happy Celebration of the goal's completion and, more importantly, convinces one of the need for completion of the *next* worthy long-term goal.

The Ability to Stand Out from the Crowd

The truly successful have the ability to be real visionaries. They stand out from the crowd and are able to achieve the unimaginable by never wavering from their ultimate goal. Imagine having a dream to become something or achieve something very special. Imagine also that this dream began, as so often happens, at a very young age, and that it becomes a never-ending urge to succeed at that particular accomplishment.

I believe the subconscious mind in these special visionaries is etched with their dream or goal. Picture a slab of granite hanging on your bedroom wall with your special dream or goal to achieve engraved and spelled out on it. You will see it every night before you close your eyes. And you will read it the moment you open your eyes each morning.

This must be what happens to an intensely driven individual who ultimately achieves his lifelong dream. The "granite" for these individuals is actually their subconscious mind. Their subconscious, each and every morning and night, flashes brightly like a neon sign. It flashes their intensely desired goal, and all during their days, the neon-sign subconscious automatically flashes in full detail what they most certainly want to achieve. It really is as simple as that.

What is it *you* want to etch into your own subconscious? Remember, it cannot be just a wish or something you may like. It must be something that you *must* do and *will* do. Planning and carrying out a wedding from the thinking stage to the completion of the honeymoon is a valid goal. Also, becoming an attorney or a doctor is a valid all-consuming goal.

This book I am writing word by word is my all-consuming goal right now and will be until its completion some three years after the thinking stage and information-compiling began. I have this urgency to give back to society. My goal is to help people to help themselves. Maybe my urgency comes from my observations over the past few years. We all have choices in our lives. We can put off many or all things we would like to accomplish. It is, after all, our life, our goal, our choice. Or we can let the all-consuming desire propel us forward toward our goal.

While exercising on my stationary bike one day, I was reading some of *Tuesdays with Morrie*, the book I mentioned earlier about a college professor, Morrie Schwartz, who was dying, and his former student, Mitch Albom, who was doing a story and compiling notes about the professor's last lessons on life and his dealing with imminent death.

When the subject of regrets came up, Morrie responded, "It's what everyone worries about, isn't it? What if today were my last day on earth?" He went on to say:

Mitch, the culture doesn't encourage you to think about such things until you're almost about to die. We're so wrapped up with egotistical things, career, family, having enough money, meeting the mortgage, getting a new car, fixing the radiator when it breaks—we're involved in trillions of little acts just to keep going. So we don't get into the habit of standing back and looking at our lives and saying, "Is this all? Is this all I want? Is something missing?" You need something to probe you in that direction. It won't just happen automatically.

After reading that passage from Morrie, the professor who had a death sentence at that time, I looked over at my new guitar, which I had neglected for the past few months and had not yet learned to play. It appeared to be nothing more than a good-looking guitar, an instrument that, if put into the right hands, could bring forth the finest sounds. But as it stared back at me, it became a reminder of what could be.

Morrie reminded me, in Mitch's book, that things should not be put off. So at that very moment, I vowed that I would teach myself how to play that tough guitar instrument—but I would do it only after finishing this book. That will be an intense goal, to learn one song really well. But as we all have choices in life, I choose to tackle the guitar at a later date. In the meantime, I will keep it right next to my exercise bike so it can stare right back at me, reminding me of the promise I made to it.

We might have an intense drive about something, but the important thing is to maintain the drive toward that one goal. It is paramount not to wander, not to have a great many goals, and not to juggle them all at the same time. There are many individuals who have had much more energy, contacts, and intelligence than I do, but who have not had any great accomplishments. Even talent, energy, and connections will not guarantee success. I have learned over many years that one must focus and commit all energies, working hard and long to see that one magic dream at a time comes to reality, programming one's own mind to never stop charging after that all-important goal and to not be deterred.

The successful individual also keeps himself fired up and motivated with positive affirmations such as this one:

I feel healthy. I feel happy. I feel terrific. I like myself, I like myself.

I will be successful. It is inevitable because my aggressiveness will lead to my success. I can, I will, I want to. All things are possible through belief in myself and the Lord; and with His help I can accomplish anything...

This is just an example of a positive success affirmation I repeat to myself on a daily basis. It is one of a few affirmations that run much longer, ones I have repeated for many years now, and one of which was shared earlier in this book.

For over thirty years, I have used affirmations as my way of staying focused, on track, and driven, while shielding myself from and eliminating the negativity that bombards each and every one of us at various turns in life.

The truly successful have a way of maintaining their positive edge. Every successful Olympic champion and great inventor hears all the same negatives we do. But the highly successful stop the negatives from penetrating their all-powerful subconscious mind.

Let me emphasize this point. The great achievers in life will never allow *anyone or anything* to rain on their parade. No matter what happens, no matter how many failures they encounter, they happily march forward with blinders on. They can only see one thing. They focus on the finish line. The finish line is *all that matters* to the extremely driven individual.

The writer Bernie Charles Forbes once said:

Life is simply a matter of concentration: You are what you set out to be. You are a composite of the things you say, the books you read, the thoughts you think, the company you keep, and the things you desire to become.

Forbes was a Scottish financial journalist and author of several books. He also founded *Forbes* magazine.

> # We Are Each Born into This
> # World Destined for Greatness!

Louis Waterman of Brooklyn, New York, invented the first capillary feed in fountain pens. Today the famous Waterman pens are recognized for high quality.

In 1884, Louis Waterman was an insurance broker. One day a new pen leaked all over a contract he was trying to sell someone. He wound up losing the insurance sale. But Waterman went back to the drawing board and perfected a new fountain pen and had it patented. He became very successful with his new invention.

Sometimes success does not come until much later in one's life. For some, the early years hold failure after failure, frustration after frustration. Many people get accustomed to the mediocrity of their lives, the average results they produce, thus thinking that real success is far beyond their reach. Then there are those who get a magical wake-up call and achieve success beyond all imagination. What these very special achievers did not realize early on was this: Greatness was always within them. Greatness is within the reach of each one of us.

If greatness is truly within the reach of each of us, then why does it not come forth in some for many years, or not at all? I believe that in some great achievers there must be complete failure in their lives first. They must reach the end of their rope before something triggers the "desire button" and turns on that all-consuming desire to succeed far beyond most others around them.

The real lesson is this: The desire button is deep inside all of us. It will never ever be activated in many people because, quite honestly, it is just too easy to leave it untouched and go through life with an inactive desire button. That is not to say that many people with inactive desire buttons don't do well in life. Many individuals lead comfortable lives. They may earn a fair wage and raise lovely families. But my point is this: If those same people would only activate that all-important desire button, they would achieve phenomenal success unreached by many. There are many people who activated the desire button later in life. Let's look at a couple:

There was Milo C. Jones, the founder of the famous Jones Pork Sausages. He was a middle-aged, poor Wisconsin farmer who suddenly became paralyzed and bedridden. It was only then that he used his mind and the physical assistance of his family to start the Jones Pork Sausage business. It was a hit.

Ray Kroc was a milkshake-mixer salesman, barely able to make ends meet. He used to sell to restaurants. He befriended the McDonald brothers at their one small hamburger stand and convinced them to allow him to franchise their business. In his late fifties, Kroc turned the one-stand operation into a multimillion-dollar business.

Welcome every morning with a smile. Look on the new day as another special gift from the Creator. Another golden opportunity to complete what you were unable to finish yesterday. Be a self-starter. Let your first hour set the theme of success and positive action that is certain to echo through your entire day. Today will never happen again. Don't waste it with a false start or no start at all. You were not born to fail.

—**Og Mandino** (1923-1996), American motivational author

Desire Leads to Success

When he was still a boy, Og Mandino's mother dropped dead in their kitchen right in front of him. Og passed on college to join the Army and became a bombardier pilot. After the war, he married and had a daughter. He had trouble paying the bills with a young family, sold insurance, and became an alcoholic. He destroyed his marriage, traveled the country, and couldn't hold down a job.

With his last thirty dollars in hand, he contemplated buying a handgun in a Cleveland pawnshop he had passed and taking his own life. Instead, he walked on and wound up in a local library. He sat down and began reading self-help books and decided at that moment to change his life.

He went to work as a salesman for W. Clement Stone, the author of one of the self-help books he had read. He quickly rose through the ranks and began writing for the company. Og's mother had always told him that he would be a great writer; this remained in his mind for many years. Years later, Og began working as the editor for W. Clement Stone's new self-help magazine, *Success Unlimited*. The rest is known history. Og penned a small book, *The Greatest Salesman in the World,* which went on to sell many millions of copies in many languages.

Og became the most-read self-help author in the world. He penned twenty-two books and has sold nearly forty million copies. His books are easy to read and will motivate one to improve his life. I have read all of his books. Unfortunately, Og passed away in the 1990s.

Og proves to us that success brews within each of us, that we can turn on that intense-desire button when we are prepared to get serious and stick with it. Og was convinced that he could be a great writer one day because his mother realized that her son had a special talent and made sure that thought was etched into Og's mind. Later in life, knowing he had a talent, Og came up with a very unique type of book to communicate his self-help messages to the reader. When he was ready to press his own intense-desire button, there was no stopping him.

Chapter Fifteen

The Never-Ending Will to Succeed Greatly

For a true writer each book should be a beginning where he tries again for something that is beyond attainment. He should always try for something that has never been done or that others have tried and failed. Then sometimes, with great luck, he will succeed.

—**Ernest Hemingway** (1899-1961), American writer and journalist

What a great quote from Ernest Hemingway! It comes from his acceptance speech after being awarded the 1954 Nobel Prize for Literature.

I remember reading that particular quote from Hemingway's speech some years ago. I printed out the quote, posted it all around my office. Then I decided to take Hemingway up on his writing advice. After all, who better to take writing advice from? So, for my sixth writing endeavor, a fiction thriller entitled *The Psychic Boy Detective*, I decided to leave my comfort zone and try "something that is beyond attainment"!

For the first time ever, I wrote a book that revolved around a twelve-year-old boy; but harder still, I told the story in first-person through the boy's mother, a forty-year-old. So I had to write as if I were a woman, but I also had to delve deeply into a twelve-year-old boy's head for all the emotions he was going through and feeling after he began receiving visions from various dead people.

I stood fast and would not waver in my writing. After all, I had Hemingway's confidence and success to prove that it could be done. If Hemingway could achieve such great success, then why couldn't I at least succeed in this one challenge he had put forth to all writers in 1954?

Well, the rest is history. I did succeed in penning a very captivating page-turner of a novel. Though it was difficult, I would not give in to my many feelings of doubt that arose during the three-and-a-half years it took from thinking stage to final, finished, and edited manuscript.

Never, ever tell me that something is impossible, because at that precise moment I will commit to the successful outcome of such a challenge!

Writing a book is similar to someone committing to four years of night school to achieve a degree of some sort. The commitment is similar and the mindset much the same, in which you never stop until you achieve the goal, the finish line. Oh, sure, it may take me five years to complete a book, or for the night-schooler to complete the credits required to graduate, but we never stop focusing on that finish line. We all have had some special goal that we have achieved. It may or may not be a "monumental" achievement. It may not be important or impressive to other people, but it is special to you. My point is that since we have already achieved success for smaller goals, we can expand the same principle and apply it to larger goals.

We Are Each Born into This World Destined for Greatness!

Michael Dell, the founder of Dell Computers, is worth $2.3 billion today. Over twenty-five years ago, Dell, a college dropout, came up with the computer giant. He resides in Austin, Texas, and has survived the past quarter-century of good times and bad. Dell is an American-made and self-made success. He has been a great inspiration to millions of people, showing that education alone does not bring success, that a powerful drive and desire to succeed can outweigh education any day of the week.

Far better it is to dare mighty things, to win glorious triumphs even though checkered by failure, than to rank with those poor spirits who neither enjoy nor suffer much because they live in the gray twilight that knows neither victory nor defeat.

—**Theodore Roosevelt** (1858-1919),
26th President of the United States

Creating the Intensely Driven Goal

So, you are reading about people who have achieved greatness. They have succeeded in reaching and accomplishing great goals. Some or most have overcome great obstacles on the rough road that leads to the finish line of a great goal. I have explained that all of us have within ourselves the ability to achieve greatness, that it is only our minds that limit the degree of greatness we can achieve.

Also, it must be remembered that we each have in our past achieved smaller but still significant goals, and that the formula is quite similar for achieving longer and more substantial goals. Every marathon runner achieves a substantial goal the second he crosses the finish line after more than twenty-six miles. What a great undertaking it is, from the planning stage, throughout the training that leads up to the race, right up to the precise moment he crosses the finish line. It doesn't matter how long it took him or what ranking he finished with. The goal was set and achieved, and that fact can now be celebrated.

There are people who take all day to build a rock garden…and those who plan on sodding an entire yard during the day…and those who undertake wallpapering an entire kitchen or bedroom. Greatness happens in each one of those endeavors, though they may seem small in scale compared to running a marathon. There is the thinking stage concerning the goal, the planning stage and garnering the materials and tools, and the stage of psyching oneself up to carry out the work that needs to be done all day long to get to the all-important finish line. There is also the positive visualization of the finished project: Picturing the finish line, well before one arrives there, is very important.

And then, of course, there is the "happy celebration" in one's own mind after achieving the goal. That is very important. That achievement celebration lasts in the mind for some time. It is that achievement reached that reinforces the confidence in us that we are worthwhile and special, and that we can achieve what we set out to do. It convinces us that we can even achieve larger goals the next time we want to.

Achieving That Goal

It is essential to plan in order to achieve anything worthwhile in life. We will never simply happen to trip over a bucket of gold, but must in fact work toward it.

Therefore, here are a few simple steps to use when planning:

1. Contemplate carefully on a specific goal.
2. Write out the special goal in full detail.
3. Make sure you understand the goal and that it is a goal you truly desire to achieve.
4. Wait one full day, contemplating the goal during this twenty-four-hour "programming time," as your mind slowly accepts what it is you are planning to accomplish.
5. If you still feel powerfully strong about that particular goal in its entirety, then write out a full page of why you want to achieve the goal. Write out exactly what it would mean to you and how it would change your present circumstances or life in any way.
6. Type out the goal summary in one simple paragraph. Post copies of the typed summary at work, in your bedroom, on your night stand, in your car, on your refrigerator, and anywhere else you will see it during your waking hours.

7. Tell everyone you can about this special goal you so desire, and how long it will take for you to achieve it.

Let's assume that your goal is to earn a law degree by attending night school. Make sure you research how long it will take you and commit to that time frame when you tell everyone about your goal.

If you desire to write a book, spell out how many pages you expect it to be. Then search and download from the Internet a picture of what you would like the front cover to look like. Next, find an old paperback book, tape the new picture over the cover of the old book, then type out a label of a tentative title for your book and tape it to the new cover you have created. Make sure to keep the prototype copy of what you believe your book will look like in plain sight for all to see, because once you commit to yourself and all around you that you will be writing a new book, and you even have a prototype cover and name, it will be nearly impossible to back down from the goal. Just like the immigrant who leaves his country to come to America, you must succeed.

People wonder how a foreigner coming to America can open a business, make money here, and become successful. You see, the immigrants make up their minds to succeed. The goal is etched deeply into their subconscious minds. They know only one thing—they will come to America, the land of opportunity; they will work endlessly and succeed greatly. The same immigrants, before setting out for America, told all their family members that they were going to America, would become successful, and would send for each of them one by one after having done so, so that they, too, could come to America. In short, the word *failure* never enters the immigrants' minds. Their goal is simple: They must succeed and send for their family because their family back home is counting on them. Back home, their family is bragging that their relative is in America, making a name for himself, and it won't be long before he sends for them.

Great expectations! It really is a mindset. We could each, if we so desired, switch roles with the foreigner. We could commit to go to their country, learn their language, and become tremendously successful ourselves in their land.

Every person who wins in any undertaking must be willing to cut all sources of retreat. Only by doing so can one be sure of maintaining that state of mind known as a burning desire to win which is one of the essentials to success.

—**Napoleon Hill** (1883-1970), American author

One great success story is the story of Napoleon Hill, who was born in 1883. His mother died when he was nine years old. Hill's father remarried, and Hill's new stepmother was a tremendous motivating force behind this young man. Hill grew up poor, raised in a two-room cabin, but he had a great imagination. Martha, his stepmother, instilled in the young boy that he could become a great writer. At age fifteen, Napoleon Hill started writing as a reporter for a small local newspaper in Wiss County, Virginia. In 1908, an amazing thing happened: Hill was assigned to interview one of the richest and most successful men in the world, the steel tycoon Andrew Carnegie.

Carnegie was seventy-three at the time, and he asked Napoleon Hill, only age 25, if he would accept a long-term assignment that Carnegie would orchestrate. Hill was instructed to interview over five hundred successful and wealthy men and women. He was asked to formulate the principles that led to the success of these great individuals. Carnegie told Hill that he would not compensate him except for reimbursement of expenses, but agreed to introduce Hill to each of the very successful individuals.

Of course, Napoleon Hill accepted the assignment. He was free to accomplish it on his own time—in the end, it took a full twenty years. He called his findings *The Philosophy of Achievement*, and the rest is history. Hill went on to become one of the most prolific self-help writers of all time. Penning many books, he was recognized early on for the book *Think and Grow Rich*. Most of his books are still available today, including *Success through a Positive Mental Attitude*, which changed my life when I first read it at age twenty-one.

Hill's interviewees included Edison, Bell, Eastman, Ford, Woolworth, and Theodore Roosevelt. The following are two of Hill's quotes:

Cherish your visions and your dreams as they are the children of your soul, the blueprints of your ultimate achievements.

and

Desire is the starting point of all achievement, not a hope, not a wish, but a keen pulsating desire which transcends everything.

How fantastic is it that words written on a page can change someone's life forever! Words can turn a failure into a tremendous success. I wonder how many people have been as positively touched as I have been by Napoleon Hill's books and his powerful words.

Andrew Carnegie was once asked, in the early 1900s, how it was possible that he had so many millionaires (forty-three at one point) working for him. He answered: "Dealing with people is a lot like digging for gold: When you go digging for an ounce of gold, you have to move tons of dirt. But when you go digging, you don't go looking for the dirt; you go looking for the gold."

The Gold, the Good, the Positive. Just as a person can become a success with the right series of words—the Gold—a person can be destroyed for a lifetime with a wrong series of words—Daggers to the Heart.

Og Mandino, the great self-help author who, early on, contemplated ending his life but, instead, opted to study Hill's great works in that library, is one such example of someone so touched.

Let's look more closely at Carnegie. The great Andrew Carnegie, by taking young Napoleon Hill under his wing and having him interview five hundred great and successful contacts, set in motion something monumental. Napoleon Hill was able to formulate a template for success that would be shared with many millions of readers over the course of many decades.

So, how many millions of people changed their lives because of Napoleon Hill's book, which was, in turn, a direct reflection of Carnegie's brilliant idea? Surely Carnegie had a pretty good idea of what would result from Hill's special interviews. He knew the project would take many years and very hard work on Hill's part. But he knew Hill could do it. And look at the lasting impact Carnegie had on this world!

You see, motivation and enthusiasm are contagious. If we send out into the work force one thousand highly motivated and positive individuals, how many people could they impact and affect? Remember that you are on a stage. Each and every day there are people watching you. A few of you, depending on your occupation, may have hundreds or even, at times, thousands of people watching, studying, analyzing, and, ultimately, maybe imitating what they see and hear you do.

Of course, we each have our own mind, but I contend that many of us are great and habitual followers, maybe because it is easier to imitate than to forge our own way, cutting our own path through the dense forest of our lives.

If you think you are beaten, you are.
If you think you dare not, you don't.
If you like to win but think you can't,
It's almost a cinch you won't.

If you think you'll lose, you're lost.
For out in the world we find
Success begins with a fellow's will
It's all in the state of mind.

If you think you are outclassed, you are.
You've got to think high to rise.
You've got to be sure of yourself before
You can ever win the prize.

Life's battles don't always go
To the stronger or faster man.
But sooner or later, the man who wins
Is the man who thinks he can.

—**C. W. Longenecker**, poet

Today's Inspiring People

As long as people have dreams—intense desires to succeed at something that to others may seem impossible—we will have those who achieve greatness. Those great achievers then inspire all the other individuals who struggle to get through their average days. We look to the immensely successful individuals to give us inspiration, motivation, hope for the future, and, more importantly, the all-powerful confidence that we, too, can excel; that we, too, can achieve what was previously believed to be "the impossible dream." The confidence we derive from an average person becoming a billionaire in a few short years becomes etched into our minds and propels us forward through thick and thin, through all the obstacles we face on our long, hard journey to ultimate success. And if we should fail to accomplish our lofty goals, as we may, we will have accomplished far more with our positive mindset than we would have if we had not been so powerfully influenced.

James Allen, the great inspirational writer from 1900 and author of the great self-help book *As a Man Thinketh*, said:

Rely upon your own judgment; be true to your own conscience; follow the light that is within you; all outward lights are so many will-o'-the-wisps. There will be those who tell you that you are foolish; that your judgment is faulty; that your conscience is all awry; and that the light within you is darkness; but heed them not. If what they say is true, the sooner you as a searcher of wisdom find it out, the better, and you can only make that discovery by bringing your powers to the test. Therefore, pursue your course bravely.

Oprah Winfrey

One of our present-day great achievers is Oprah Winfrey. Born on January 29, 1954, in Mississippi, Oprah was sexually abused as a child. She moved to Nashville and, in 1974, began working in broadcasting.

In 1976, Oprah moved to Baltimore, where she hosted a TV show called "People Are Talking." She was twenty-two and stayed with the show for eight years. Then she was hired by a TV station out of Chicago to host her own morning show.

In 1986, Oprah launched her own nationally televised show, and the rest is history. It has been said that Oprah was the richest African-American of the twentieth century. She has starred in numerous films, won many awards, and is world-renowned and much loved.

Oprah spent her own money to start a $40 million school for four hundred fifty girls in Africa, where her students would have an opportunity to have the best education and go on to higher education, all in a very poor country where few have the opportunity to excel.

Oprah has published books and even has her own magazine, called "O." In her book, *O's Guide to Life: The Best of O, The Oprah Magazine*, published by Oxmoor House, Oprah says, "Every sunrise is like a new page, a chance to rescue each day in all its glory."

In her book, Oprah also speaks about her poor upbringing and her intense desire when she says, "I remember being fifteen years old, standing in the drugstore three corners from my house, waiting for the September issue of *Seventeen* [magazine] to arrive. I was a faithful reader all through my teens, until I turned 18, but the back-to-school issue was the most anticipated, and I couldn't risk having it sell out. I never had enough money at one time to buy a subscription, but I would sacrifice two school lunches a month for the 50 cents to buy the magazine filled with spectacular fashion, ideas, and dreams. It gave me hope that one day I could live like the girls in those pages."

It is true that we are what we think about on a consistent basis. Oprah clearly was a driven person with a dream. That dream resonated deep within her for years. She had vision. Oprah wanted to be a success. But more importantly, Oprah *visualized* herself as a success. It was just a question of when, and of what form that success would take.

Tripping the Circuit Breaker

We each have the ability, deep within, to achieve phenomenal success in life. But many people will never achieve their greatest, loftiest goals because they keep tripping the circuit breaker in their minds and shutting down the intense desire to achieve those goals.

There have been many inventors who failed to succeed in completing a successful working invention when they were *so close*. They yielded to another inventor who was clearly behind in experiments and working prototypes, but the lead inventor tripped that negative circuit breaker in his subconscious, the one that convinces us that we can succeed, the one that drives us to work on, though we are faced with failure after failure. The circuit breaker in our minds works just like the circuit breaker in your home—it shuts down when there is an overload of power. And tripping it is much like throwing in the towel in a prize fight.

We've all succeeded at small goals in life, mostly taken for granted as insignificant. But I stress that our intense desire to succeed carried us to the finish line of those goals.

In each successful accomplishment the circuit breaker in our subconscious mind does not get tripped into the "off" position. But we also have most likely had larger and smaller goals where we have tripped that circuit breaker, which in turn stopped our momentum and drive toward that worthwhile goal. So we know the mechanics behind failure. We know, too, the mechanics that will lead to success.

My tripping of that circuit breaker after just a few weeks of trying to learn the new guitar I had purchased. I clearly flipped that circuit breaker into the "off" position, convincing myself that I would start up again in the future and learn the guitar then. Failure? Yes. Will I one day succeed? Maybe. I would have to start over.

But an intense, burning desire, in order to get you to the finish line, must be maintained from early on in the thinking and planning stages, and on through all the obstacles and small failures you may encounter along the long road to the achievement of that important goal.

Look once more at the New York City marathon runner. Take, for example, the person who never ran before and got the idea, maybe a year and a half before the more than 26-mile race, to do so. As with any worthwhile goal, the marathon runner would have to plan for success. Planning would involve diet, training, commitment to run, and allocation of time each day or week to work out. The road to that achievement would be very long. There might be injuries, a lot of pain, and setbacks. There might be perhaps hundreds of moments of self-doubt, of frustration, of agony—plenty of times when that circuit breaker in the runner's subconscious mind could be tripped into the "off" position.

I would venture to estimate that for every one hundred people with the goal of becoming a new marathon racer and training for one and a half years, only a percentage of the people with that first inclination to run would see it through to the end. Though there would surely be some circumstances beyond the runners' control, many non-finishers merely flipped the circuit breaker.

If someone offered you $1 million to train for and run in that 26.2-mile marathon one-and-a-half years from now, do you think you could complete the race? Absolutely! So could I, bad knee and all; I'd manage somehow to walk, crawl, or skip across that finish line!

And here is an important point: The never-ending, intense desire to achieve that specific million-dollar goal would never cease to propel you forward for the full year-and-a-half it took. Amazing, isn't it? Motivation works in strange ways.

Chapter Sixteen

The Hot-Iron Branding of Enthusiasm

You brought something to the planet that was not here before you showed up. And if you don't bring it out, if you don't develop it, we will all suffer.

—**Les Brown** (b. 1945), Motivational speaker

To protect their livestock from cattle rustlers, cattlemen would put their own markings onto their cattle by branding them. This guaranteed that, if the cattle were stolen, they could prove which were their own cattle.

Similarly, we can put our own enthusiasm-branding into the subconscious minds of other individuals. This enthusiasm can last within other individuals for their lifetime.

Attitude is paramount when we discuss the long road to success. Without maintaining a positive attitude throughout the long journey, we will never achieve success. It is the powerful emotion of enthusiasm that carries us forward and across the finish line of any worthwhile goal—indeed, that carries us through a lifetime of success. We each have choices in life. We choose a positive or a negative attitude. We choose to be enthusiastic or blasé. And we subconsciously choose failure or success. Because we radiate our emotions to everyone with whom we come in contact, we, in turn, can influence others with our enthusiasm and zest for life, or tear others down with a negative attitude. We may not be fully aware of what we are projecting to others.

Sometimes our attitudes are influenced by all the actions and activities we encounter each day. But our attitude is still our *choice*, and that must remain in the forefront of our conscious mind. The enthusiastic person clearly stands out from all others. The enthusiastic person attracts others the way a light source attracts insects. And over time, it is the truly enthusiastic person who has a lasting effect on other individuals.

Let me give you an example:

At age twenty-one, I became a life insurance representative for a very small insurance company. I was the youngest agent in the office. At age twenty-three, I was promoted and became the youngest sales manager, a role in which I would recruit, train, and supervise new agents. Because we were a small, unknown company and couldn't pay high weekly training allowances, we couldn't attract the best sales trainees. We would wind up hiring young people in their early twenties who had no real sales experience. In sales jobs of any type, more than 80 percent fail in the first three years.

I had hired three twenty-year-old agents, one female and two males, all with other things on their minds than selling insurance and making a career out of insurance sales. They each lasted a couple of years and then left our company. One of the men moved on to another major company, then left and stopped selling life insurance but started his own successful property-and-casualty business. I lost contact with the other male. But the female also remained in insurance sales. Today, some thirty years later, two out of the three are very successful. I believe that my enthusiasm and early training helped mold them and has stayed with them all these years later.

I am convinced that we each can be branded deep within our subconscious and that such enthusiasm can last a lifetime if we choose to maintain it. This is what happened to me as a new twenty-one-year-old agent. After three months of struggling to sell life insurance, I attended a seminar and listened to motivational speaker and Olympic gold medal winner Bob Richards. He so inspired me that afternoon with his motivating speech that I was positively infected with his tremendous enthusiasm. That day was the first day of my new journey to success. I never looked back. Thirty-four years later, I am still fired up with enthusiasm. I was branded by the motivational speaker, but I also had to maintain that enthusiasm, which I did by continually studying self-help books to stay positive. So, we can influence someone for life, but only if they want to maintain and feed upon that deep-seated enthusiasm in their own subconscious.

The opposite also is true. Someone can, in fact, be branded with negative thoughts, and this, too, can be etched into the subconscious. It also can be maintained by continued negative thought impulses. So watch what you feed to that powerful computer-brain of yours. And watch, too, what impulses you send out to all who come in contact with you. It is your choice. It is your right to think and act and project enthusiasm—or negative vibes. What a fabulous legacy it would be to have your enthusiasm positively branded on another individual the way Bob Richards affected me that day some thirty-four years ago!

This book you are reading can change your life—but only if you will allow it to happen, only if you convince your subconscious mind that it is now time to make a change and to never look back. Remember, you can have anything you truly desire. Any goal will be yours—but only if you never, ever stop wanting, working towards, and visualizing the successful achievement of that goal.

Every great and commanding movement in the annals of the world is the triumph of enthusiasm.

—**Ralph Waldo Emerson** (1803-1882),
American philosopher, essayist, poet

The Powerful Burning Desire to Succeed

We can program our minds for success. A computer program instructs a computer to carry out a series of specific tasks. Programs can do almost anything, from intricate math calculations to analyzing data and sorting words. There is even a software program that recognizes your specific voice and types the words you say fairly rapidly, almost like your own secretary inside your computer.

Well, the computer inside your brain is far more powerful than any man-made computer that exists.

The brain has many functions, some of which are:

- It controls blood pressure, heart, and body temperature.
- It analyzes data from all the senses—such as seeing, smelling, tasting, hearing, and feeling.
- It controls everything that the manufacturing plant of the body asks of it, such as sleeping, walking, running, swimming, sitting, balancing, sports, and so much more.

Some other intriguing aspects of the brain are:

- The brain uses 20 percent of your body's energy, yet it makes up only 2 percent of your body's weight.
- The weight of the average human brain is only three pounds.
- There are over one hundred thousand miles of blood vessels in the brain.
- There are one hundred billion neurons in the human brain.
- The average person uses less than 10 percent of the capacity of the brain.

If you can program your brain with certain commands, the brain will work to carry forth the desired outcome. We don't fully understand the human brain, but we know that it is more powerful than even one thousand computers linked together.

The Unending Desire to Achieve

I've missed more than nine thousand shots in my career. I've lost almost three hundred games. Twenty-six times I've been trusted to take the game-winning shot and missed. I've failed over and over and over again in my life. And that is why I succeed.

—**Michael Jordan** (b. 1963), Retired American pro basketball player

Michael Jordan was the best basketball player who ever played the game. He won six NBA championships, scored over 32,000 points, and won two Olympic gold medals. Jordan earned over $800 million playing basketball. He was a tremendous success in sports and in life. But he wasn't a natural ball player. He wasn't an instant success. Quite the opposite; Jordan was considered a below-par player in his early days. So what happened? How did Jordan become the greatest basketball player of all time?

Michael Jordan started playing basketball for Laney High School in Wilmington, North Carolina. He was 5'11" and skinny when the school cut the mediocre player from the high school team. But soon after that, Jordan began to play differently. It was as if he reinvented himself and played a new type of basketball. He was nicknamed "Air Jordan" because he could almost magically hang in the air as he made unbelievable basketball shots, astounding the best players in the game.

It was as if Jordan said, "Okay, show me how the game is played and I will change my game so I will outplay everyone and win."

The intense desire to win made Jordan the best. He would not stop until he was recognized as the best in the game.

The Magic of Desire

At age twenty-three, as the youngest sales manager of the insurance company I worked for, I desired more. I can remember each year, at the company's annual awards ceremony, when I would just miss being granted the Sales Manager of the Year Award.

I always got beaten out by a very talented sales manager. I so desired that award, which resembled the prestigious Academy Award, that I made it my mission to raise my game to a higher level and have my staff of sales people sell more than ever before.

But right at that time I had a larger dream. I wanted to be promoted to the top spot of District Manager of the entire sales office. So one day, when the vice-president of the company came to our district office for a branch meeting, young John Carinci approached him. I walked up to him and said, "Mr. Posa, one day you will be promoting me to District Manager of this office. I don't know exactly when, but I do know that I will be promoted and run this office for you."

Less than two years later, I was promoted by the vice-president to District Manager, in charge of the entire staff of fifteen people. At age twenty-seven, I was the youngest District Manager the company had ever had. And in the very first year as District Manager, I won the prestigious President's Star Award and had four of the agents of my district also win awards.

You see, I had a burning desire to succeed. I had a dream that would not die. It was so important to me that I had to boldly inform the vice-president of it. And, of course, once you make such a bold prediction to such an important man, there can be no such thing as failing.

That desire to win the District Manager promotion was the first thing I thought about each morning and the last thing I thought about before falling off to sleep each night. I was super-charged. There was nothing that would stop me from succeeding.

The principle is the same for all the different goals each of us has. We can each succeed if we desire something as much.

Desire to Win an Olympic Gold Medal

Dan Jansen was a great speed skater. He took up skating after being inspired by his sister, Jane. In 1984, Dan finished sixteenth in the 1,000 meters at the 1984 Olympics.

In the 1988 Olympics, Jansen was favored to win a gold medal in the 500- and 1,000-meter speed-skating competition. He had worked four years at perfecting his skating and was all set. But on the day of the Olympic race, Jansen received a call saying that his sister, Jane, was dying of leukemia. He spoke to his sister that day, but she was unable to speak to him. A short time later that morning, Dan Jansen was informed that his sister had passed away.

Jansen was determined to race that same day. He, of course, wanted to bring home the gold medal from that Olympic race. But, as determined as he was, Dan Jansen fell in the 500-meter race, as well as in the 1,000-meter race. He went home with no medals from the 1988 Olympics.

In the 1992 Olympic games, Jansen was once again favored to win. But again, he left the Olympics with no medals. He finished well out of the running.

So, in his final Olympic games in 1994, Dan Jansen had to stay highly motivated and at the top of his game. The desire to succeed had been etched deeply in his subconscious mind for at least four thousand days. Jansen had to stay in tip-top shape, and for all that time he had to maintain that intense desire to win at a sport where a simple slip meant waiting another four years. Perseverance pays off. In 1994, competing in his last Olympics, Jansen won the 1,000-meter race at Lillehammer, Norway.

Great spirits have often encountered violent opposition from mediocre minds.

—**Albert Einstein** (1878-1955), Physicist and philosopher

Great Visionaries Have Changed Our World

I have always been intrigued by the great inventors of the past. Inventors are visionaries who take a concept or a dream, mold and perfect the picture in their minds, and then attack it until it has been brought into reality.

An inventor has a super-charged subconscious mind that works tirelessly in overdrive. Success to an inventor is inevitable; the failures all along the way, along with numerous roadblocks, are almost happily accepted. You see, the great inventors realize that failures will present themselves many times. Failure never throws inventors. Rather, it spurs them on. Each failure energizes the great inventors because they realize that they are that much closer to the working model of their invention.

Since the beginning of time, humanity has been reinventing itself. Each generation that replaces our forefathers seems, almost magically, to improve on all things in our lives.

Look at the wheel, the first crude tool, the weapons used to hunt, and technology. What the mind of man can dream up, it can bring forth to reality. We dreamt of flying in a metal object in the air. Then we dreamt of a rocket ship that could fly to the moon, and then farther along to Mars.

The person with a positively reinforced subconscious mind can accomplish greatness. But it must be stressed here that the powerful subconscious mind must be routinely reinforced and energized with the proper programming. This alone is the main difference between mediocre results and those who achieve true greatness.

Remember, we each are reinvented and improved results of those great minds and people who have preceded us.

Let's look at some great inventions:

The air conditioner was invented in Norway in 1902 by Erik Rotheim.

Aspirin was invented in 1897 by Felix Hoffmann in Germany. It still is saving many heart attack victims every day.

The computer was invented in 1939 by John V. Atanasoff and Clifford E. Berry of the U.S.A. The first computers were huge and far less powerful than the hand-held computers we now use every day. They've been reinvented and improved many times over, based on dreams!

In 1867, dynamite was patented by Alfred Nobel.

The refrigerator was invented in 1842 by John Gorrie. Until that time, and even for years afterward, people purchased blocks of ice and had them delivered to their homes placed in an ice box to keep some foods cold.

In 1958, someone even reinvented the already present roller skate. They improved the concept into a new form of transport called a skateboard. I even had one in the 1960s. It was invented by Bill and Mark Richards in the U.S.A. Brilliant? You bet! Reinvention of an inspired dream!

The first mobile phone was brought about in 1946 by Bell Laboratories.

The phonograph was Thomas Edison's dream in 1877. Thomas Edison was interviewed by the *New York Times* in 1908. He was asked to predict the changes that would come about in the future. He spoke about the improvement of concrete and the architectural advancements sure to come within twenty years. He said the following:

"Moving-picture machines will be so perfected that the characters will not only move, but will speak, and all the accessories and effects of the stage will be faithfully reproduced on the living-picture stage. This, of course will not be done as well as on the regular stage, but its standard will approach very near to that, and the fact that such entertainment will be furnished for five cents will draw vast numbers of the working classes. The result will be that the masses will have the advantage of the moral of good drama, they will find an inexpensive and improving way of spending the evening, and the death knell of the saloon will be sounded."

Edison was a great visionary. Look at us today—102 years later we have a great new, advanced technological marvel. A motion picture called *Avatar* has broken all records for box office sales and will go on to gross more money than any motion picture ever before, all with new 3-D technology and exceptionally realistic characters. The film required ten years of thinking, planning, and production by James Cameron. A man with vision? Absolutely! He was an inspired reinvention of his predecessors.

> # We Are Each Born into This World Destined for Greatness!

Philo T. Farnsworth invented the television in 1927. He drastically improved the concept of prior devices which were based on unworkable technology.

In 1921, 14-year-old Philo came up with an idea while working on the family farm in Idaho. While mowing hay in rows, he realized an electron beam could scan a picture in horizontal lines, reproducing the image almost instantaneously. This laid a monumental foundation for Philo's invention of the television when he was only twenty years old.

On September 7, 1927, Farnsworth's image-dissector camera tube transmitted its first image, a simple straight line, at his laboratory. He first demonstrated his television system to the press on September 3, 1928.

You will never stub your toe standing still. The faster you go, the more chance there is of stubbing your toe, but the more chance you have of getting somewhere.

—**Charles F. Kettering** (1876-1958), American engineer, inventor

Chapter Seventeen

Life Is to Be Lived to the Fullest

No pessimist ever discovered the secret of the stars, or sailed to an uncharted land, or opened a new doorway for the human spirit.

—Helen Keller (1880-1968),
American author, political activist, lecturer

I am reminded all too often of just how short life can be. Oh, sure, I am constantly pointing out the many people who live to age 100 today. But we are never given, at the time of our birth, a certificate of guarantee that we will live to any specific age. So, life was given to you and me. The true miracle of life was bestowed upon us to be lived to the fullest.

To *not* live one's life to the max is the same as covering up a work of art so that the light and air won't fade it. Or locking up the diamond engagement ring, or a new Cadillac, for fear of its getting stolen, lost, or damaged.

We insult our Creator if we don't give life everything we have to give without holding anything back.

I firmly believe that any man's finest hour, the greatest fulfillment of all that he holds dear, is that moment when he has worked his heart out in a good cause and lies exhausted on the field of battle—victorious.

—Vince Lombardi (1913-1970), American football coach

Why do some people live on the edge, right on the brink of disaster, while others take the easy road, bypassing many opportunities all along their life's journey?

Maybe it is time to consider living dangerously. Maybe it's time to reject the commands of power, the dictates of society and public opinion, and to stop worrying about what other people think about what you do. You have the power and ability to create your own reality—to change what isn't working, and to manifest what you desire.

—**Dick Sutphen,** Author and psychic researcher

I remember the day Walt Disney died. I was a boy of eleven, living in New Jersey. On that day, December 15, 1966, I was delivering newspapers, and when I went to a particular home, a man told me Walt Disney had just died.

Walt Disney, to me, meant Mickey Mouse, the Mouseketeers, and cartoons. Little did I know at the time that Walt was one of the most elaborate visionaries of all time. Of course, he died far too early at the age of sixty-four, but Walt Disney lived his life on the edge.

Those Who Dared To Fail—in Order to Succeed

It is not the critic who counts: not the man who points out how the strong man stumbles or where the doer of deeds could have done better. The credit belongs to the man who is actually in the arena, whose face is marred by dust and sweat and blood, who strives valiantly, who errs and comes up short again and again, because there is no effort without error or shortcoming, but who knows the great enthusiasms, the great devotions, who spends himself for a worthy cause; who, at the best, knows, in the end, the triumph of high achievement, and who, at the worst, if he fails, at least he fails while daring greatly, so that his place shall never be with those cold and timid souls who knew neither victory nor defeat.

—**Theodore Roosevelt** (1858-1919), 26th President of the United States

Walt Disney clearly was the animation king of all time, the forefather of cartoon excellence and new, unique techniques. Walt, along with his brother Roy, produced animation classics. But his road to success had so many roadblocks that an average person would have abandoned all dreams way before they came to pass. Not Walt.

Born in 1901 in Chicago, Illinois, Walt started drawing as a young boy. He went on to start a small animation business out of his garage, where he worked at night after his day job. He created short cartoons in the garage on a shoestring.

Before long, Walt and Roy began a new business venture, making more cartoons together. They rented a cheap room. They ate all their meals in a cafeteria, where one brother would order a meat dish and the other would order vegetables and they would share with each other to save money.

Walt once recalled, "We cooked, ate, and slept in that one room, and had to walk about a mile before we reached the bathroom; and yet when I think back, we had a grand time in those days."

Walt's first Mickey Mouse silent film was a disaster. And when he made another Mickey movie, *Steamboat Willie*, no distributor wanted it. So Walt distributed it independently. He hit snags all along the way, even filing for bankruptcy a few times. Each new film almost put him out of business forever.

In 1927, Walt tried to get MGM to back Mickey Mouse, but he was rejected and told the idea would never work—a giant mouse on the screen would terrify women!

Yet, Walt Disney stuck with his dreams, didn't allow anyone to kill his inspiration, and ultimately succeeded beyond his wildest expectations. In the end, he received fifty-nine Academy Award nominations and won twenty-six Oscars and seven Emmy Awards. The Walt Disney Company today has annual revenues of $35 billion.

Never Give In; Never Give Up!

Only those who dare to fail greatly can achieve greatly.

—**Robert F. Kennedy** (1925-1968),
American politician and civil rights activist

When young Thomas Edison was in school, his teachers said he was "too stupid to learn anything." Yet, Edison invented the incandescent light bulb against all odds. He made over one thousand unsuccessful attempts—failures—before perfecting the world-changing invention.

Jerry Seinfeld, the award-winning comedian, executive producer, and millionaire was booed off the stage during his first stand-up comedy act. He was terrible. Of course, he could have hung it all up that very night. After all, look at the pressure of trying to make a room full of people laugh, especially as an unknown comedian. But, of course, Jerry Seinfeld went on to excel in his field.

Even Elvis Presley was fired after his very first performance at the Grand Ole Opry. He was told he had no talent.

Never give in, never give in, never, never, never, never—in nothing great or small, large or petty—never give in except to convictions of honor and good sense. Never, never, never, never give up.

—**Winston Churchill** (1874-1965), British politician

Even Bill Gates was originally written off as a failure by many people. Bill Gates, considered the world's richest man, and the founder and chairman of Microsoft, as a young man dropped out of Harvard University. Yet, he went on to prove the world wrong about him and to change the world of computers forever. You see, Bill just had to find his niche.

So, what is your niche? What fire do you have in your belly? What fires you up every day and occupies your mind more than anything else? Dream that dream! Achieve that goal! Be all you want to be!

As I have stated before, writing this book was my burning desire. I had an all-consuming desire to finish it. It was the first thing I thought of when I opened my eyes and the last thing I visualized in bed at night. I was consumed as I did research and wrote every word out in longhand.

I had written it with every spare minute I had. There was a great deal of in-depth research and time invested, but the work never once fazed me, because I was that consumed with its completion.

We cannot possibly be consumed with everything in life. That new and shiny acoustic guitar I purchased had to be put on hold. I will pick it up again sometime in the future. You see, it is not an all-consuming desire at this time.

To make sure that this book remains my all-consuming desire for the couple of years I expect it will take until its printing date, I told everyone about my undertaking it. I even posted notes on Facebook, Twitter, and every website pertaining to writers. Once I announce to the world that I am writing a new and outstanding self-help book, there is no way I can back down. Everyone I know keeps asking, "So when will it be available? How is it going so far?"

I put pressure on myself to write the best book of my life. But that is all right—I thrive on challenges. In fact, I welcome it when someone tells me I can't do something or that something is impossible. I love the impossible. All worthwhile inventions in the world were once impossible.

I still get a kick out of my very first iPod by Apple Computers. I have about eleven hundred songs on this tiny piece of metal component that measures an eighth of an inch thick and about one and a half inches wide by three inches long. Of course, my iPod is very much out-of-date, and I will be purchasing an updated model. But I am amazed. Old-fashioned albums used to be played on a record player, but I can fit approximately one hundred twenty of those old records on this mini-computer! And the new ones hold four thousand songs and full movie videos, too. As Napoleon Hill said, what the mind of man can conceive and believe it will ultimately achieve. Someone had a dream. Someone did the impossible with the iPod invention.

James Cameron just broke all records with his latest movie blockbuster, *Avatar*. He waited until the needed technology could catch up to his advanced thinking. He worked on the film for over ten years, and the outcome is that all future films such as his will use this newfound technology with which he broke ground.

We Are Each Born into This World Destined for Greatness!

Great discoveries and undertakings are the results of dedicated people who refuse to give in to failure and are not afraid of the hard work required. They stand out from the crowd and lead the way for all of us to admire.

In 2010, reconstructive-surgery expert Professor Laurent Lantieri led a team of ten surgeons at the Henri-Mondor University Hospital in Créteil, France, south of Paris, in completing a successful nineteen-hour operation—what is claimed to be the world's first full face transplant. The operation was performed on a 35-year-old man with neuro-fibromatosis, a genetic illness known colloquially as Elephant Man disease, which causes tumors to grow on nerve endings, severely disfiguring the face. Afterwards, the patient had full control over his eyelids and tear ducts. He is even growing stubble.

The very rare procedure began with a seven-hour operation to remove the face from a patient who had died just a few hours earlier. Then came a twelve-hour procedure to transplant the face onto its new owner and reconnect the veins and muscles.

Inventions, discoveries, and breakthroughs are all performed by visionaries, great people who convince us that we, too, can be great and that nothing at all is impossible.

Chapter Eighteen

What Is Motivation?

If you hear a voice in your head that says you cannot paint, then by all means paint, and that voice will be silenced.

—Vincent van Gogh (1853-1890), Dutch painter

Many people secretly wish to be more motivated about many things. Some of us wish to re-motivate ourselves about many facets of our lives. But what is motivation, really?

In the fabulous book *Success through a Positive Mental Attitude* by Napoleon Hill and W. Clement Stone, the authors define motivation as "that which induces action or determines choice. It is that which provides a motive. A motive is the 'inner urge' only within the individual which incites him to action, such as an instinct, passion, emotion, habit, mood, impulse, desire, or idea. It is the hope or other force which starts an action in an attempt to produce specific results."

Nothing in life happens by mistake. To be motivated for a long period you must work on it. For an athlete to be prepared to play Major League Baseball each year, he must attend and work hard through spring training. Spring training can last a good six weeks. All during that preparation time a baseball player makes many mistakes. His body hurts from the exercise needed to get in shape. Without the proper practice period of six weeks, the professional player could not play up to the standards expected of a Major League player.

A Major League Baseball player realizes that if he is not at the top of his game for an extended period of time, he can easily be replaced by a new and upcoming rookie hotshot player who is desperately seeking an opportunity to break into the big leagues.

Talk about pressure! That is why the salaries of Major Leaguers are so high. Maybe *we* should act like someone is standing close by, waiting for us to fail so we can be replaced. Maybe then we would be at the top of our own game on a more consistent basis.

Many of life's failures are people who did not realize how close they were to success when they gave up.

—**Thomas Edison** (1847-1931), American inventor

So, then, how do we keep ourselves motivated for an extended period? How can we rise above the mediocre and average worker? How can we excel so we may earn that promotion? How can we land that better job, or finish college and earn that long-awaited degree which will enable our growth and higher income levels?

You already know you are capable of greatness. We all are. The amazing thing is that we were each born to be great. It is only our thinking that has infected our mind with roadblocks.

Oh, sure, you may be successful, happy, well-off financially. But you also may have settled into a comfort zone that many people accept in life. We each have the capability of being outstanding, not only in one area, but in many. Are you settling? Are you merely content? Do you know in your heart that you can do far better, or do something else you have always dreamed of doing?

When I was a teen, the boy who lived next door played the guitar. He was great—very talented. He was even able to write songs. For some reason, I couldn't learn the guitar, though I tried to teach myself. So I stopped trying. It wasn't my thing.

Still, I desperately wanted to write songs. But how do you write songs without playing an instrument for the music? Well, no one ever told me that I couldn't write songs. And if my neighbor could write songs, so could I! So I wrote the words to tunes I created in my mind. Then I would sing the songs out and record them on a small tape recorder. The year was 1968. I have been writing songs ever since, singing unknown musical notes and words into tape recorders and, now, directly onto computer hard drives.

You see, my burning desire to write songs was so powerful that I overcame the obstacles before me. Over the years, I have had professional musicians listen to and decipher the tunes I was singing, and have had some of my songs recorded professionally, mostly for my own enjoyment. To this day, if inspired, I can write an entire song in less than ten minutes. My goal is to have more of them transcribed, deciphered, and made into professionally sung songs.

I will point out that my first songs were not fantastic. And some along the way were not great. But over the years I have accumulated over four hundred songs, and they have improved with every new one written.

Nothing is impossible. I can guarantee that if someone offered me one million dollars if I could only play ten full songs on the guitar by two months from now, I would be able to do it. I am sure most of us would be able to learn the new instrument and play ten songs for one million dollars. Desire is the key. I know I would be so motivated to complete that task that nothing would stop me from receiving that money.

Impossible is just a big word thrown around by small men who find it easier to live the world they've been given than to explore the power they have to change it. Impossible is not a fact. It's an opinion. Impossible is not a declaration. It's a dare. Impossible is potential. Impossible is temporary. Impossible is nothing.

—**David Beckham** (b. 1975), English footballer

Using Your Mind to Change Your Life

Your mind can change your life, but like a powerful locomotive, it must be harnessed, controlled, and maximized. Let's look deeper into the mind.

Joseph Murphy, in his book *The Power of Your Subconscious Mind,* says, "The conscious and subconscious mind: An excellent way to get acquainted with the two functions of your mind is to look upon your own mind as a garden. You are a gardener, and you are planting seeds (thoughts) in your subconscious mind all day long, based on your habitual thinking. As you sow in your subconscious mind, shall you reap in your body and environment. Begin now to sow thoughts of peace, happiness, right action, good will, and prosperity."

The human mind thinks about 3,600 thoughts per hour, 60,000 thoughts per day. It is a proven fact that most talk around us is negative. Most news we read and hear is negative. If we have sixty thousand thoughts per day, as estimated, then how can we possibly control what seeps into our brains?

Blinders to Protect Your Brain

There are so many negatives all around us that sometimes it may feel like it is impossible to forge ahead and stay positive. But there are some real fixes you can practice in your everyday living. A few things to put into practice immediately are these:

1. Put it all in perspective.
2. Take life one day at a time.
3. Use self-suggestion statements.
4. Exercise regularly to control any extra stress.
5. Be thankful for everything that is right in your life.
6. Each morning, noon, and night, visualize what you plan to accomplish, what your long-term goal or dream is.
7. Apply mental blinders to protect and shield your subconscious.

There are two days in every week about which we should not worry, two days which should be kept from fear and apprehension.

One of these days is Yesterday with all its mistakes and cares, its faults and blunders, its aches and pains. Yesterday has passed forever beyond our control. All the money in the world cannot bring back yesterday. We cannot undo a single act we performed; we cannot erase a single word we said.

Yesterday is gone forever.

The other day we should not worry about is Tomorrow with all its possible adversities, its burdens, its large promise and its poor performance; tomorrow is also beyond our immediate control. Tomorrow's sun will rise, either in splendor or behind a mask of clouds, but it will rise. Until it does, we have no stake in tomorrow, for it is yet to be born.

This leaves only one day, Today.

Any person can fight the battle of just one day. It is when you and I add the burdens of those two awful eternities—Yesterday and Tomorrow—that we break down.

It is not the experience of today that drives a person mad; it is the remorse or bitterness of something which happened yesterday and the dread of what tomorrow may bring.

Let us, therefore, live but one day at a time.

—Author unknown

Okay, so we understand that we cannot allow ourselves to get overwhelmed about life, problems, money, sickness, even love. We must keep it all in perspective, and when we do, it always seems more manageable. One day at a time is easy to conquer!

So the magic potion, then, is the power of feeding your subconscious mind. It has been proven that the subconscious mind will accept and believe that which is fed into it on a consistent basis. So if we feed it prepared statements or thoughts on a systematic basis, our subconscious mind will accept these thought impulses as facts.

Very important: Your subconscious mind will believe and act upon the thoughts it receives from the conscious mind. Your subconscious mind never sleeps. It is constantly processing and releasing back to your conscious mind thoughts that will either reinforce good feelings or reinforce negative feelings.

The mental blinders I speak about are something you consciously imagine applying. When you hear, see, or feel all the negativity around you, you effectively raise the blinders to serve as a shield by repeating positive self-suggestion affirmations. Positive self-suggestions should be custom-made, but to get you started, some I use are the following: "I feel healthy, I feel happy, I feel terrific!"

The magic in affirmations comes when you keep the statements consistent. The subconscious mind must be convinced through repetition that the statement or desire is valid.

So take a statement like, "I will finish writing this book in three months, and it will be fabulous!" This statement will be accepted, if repeated throughout the day numerous times. Then the positive impulses will be sent from your inner, subconscious mind to your conscious, outer mind. The impulses released will be like the light pulsations from a strobe light, reminding you, even when you are occupied with other things, that you *will* be finishing the new book.

You could use an affirmation such as, "I feel great, I feel accomplished, I am getting more done every day!"

My custom affirmations have not changed in many years. I have three different, very long statements which I choose from. I try to say them all to myself each and every day. It is precisely these affirmations that slowly and systematically, over time, raise the mental blinders that shield my subconscious mind from absorbing most of the negative talk, news, and actions that surround us all. I hear, see and read the same negatives every day that everyone else does, but it is as if they bounce right off the shield that has been built up to protect the inner part of my mind, the all-powerful subconscious.

Here is only a small sample of one of my personal affirmations. This one actually runs much longer in its entirety:

"I feel healthy, I feel happy, I feel terrific. I like myself, I like myself, I like myself. I will be successful; it's inevitable because my aggressiveness will lead to opportunities for my success. I can, I will, I want to. All things are possible through belief in myself and the Lord, and with His help I can accomplish anything. I feel great, I feel wonderful, I've got the world by the tail. If I start acting enthusiastic, I'll become enthusiastic. If I start acting positive, I will become positive. If I start acting happy, I will become happy. It's amazing, but when I act enthusiastic, others around me become enthusiastic. When I act positive, others around me become positive. When I act happy, others around me become happy. We have choices in life—we can act enthusiastic or blasé. I choose to act enthusiastic. We can act positive or . . ."

The statement goes on for another five minutes. It is important to stress that my statement must be repeated three times throughout the day. It has never changed and is totally memorized, as are the other two full five-minute statements.

So there you have it: my success formula for combating depression and negativity, and for accomplishing any reasonable goal or dream you may have. Many readers will be thoroughly entertained by this book, but they will not apply much of what I suggest. There will be those very few, the ones who are tired of being tired and who want to raise their success level, who will apply some of the methods described. Those few make writing a book like this all that more rewarding. Your life will change forever if you allow it to, by applying what you are reading here. And when it does, I want you to contact me and share it with me.

Remember, it is easier to follow the crowd; it is harder to clear your own path through an unknown forest.

People are always blaming their circumstances for what they are. I don't believe in circumstances. The people who get on in this world are the people who get up and look for the circumstances they want, and if they can't find them, make them.

—**George Bernard Shaw** (1856-1950), Playwright, political activist

Here is a very small portion of another self-suggestion or positive affirmation that I repeat to myself a few times a day:

"I am the greatest miracle in the world. For many years I have not acted like the greatest living miracle in the world, but now I finally realize I am. Because as the greatest living miracle, I don't allow myself to worry. The greatest living miracle realizes that 92 percent of all worry is useless and self-defeating and draining. The greatest living miracle also doesn't allow fear to get him down because as the greatest living miracle, I now realize that the Lord is my Shepherd; I shall not fear. I vow to act like the greatest living miracle in the world from here on, because now I realize that each and every day I am observed very carefully by everyone I come into contact with. And if I begin to act like the greatest living miracle in the world, then they, too, will begin to act like the greatest living miracle in the world that they are . . ."

This was just a short piece of one of my full statements. Again, it is said word for word in exactly the same order each and every day. It has worked for me for more than thirty years. Only recently has this practice begun to be more widely recognized as a worthwhile and motivating process.

If you take only one idea or motivation away after reading this book, take away the positive self-affirmations. Start out with a small custom statement, such as, "I will be successful, because I will no longer allow negative influences to affect me!" or "I am the greatest living miracle in the world. I can accomplish anything I truly desire. I will stand up and stand out, and I will be different!"

I want you to think of the inner, subconscious mind this way: The subconscious mind is similar to the sun. When you have fed positive thoughts, affirmations, and joyful actions to the subconscious, sponge-like mind, it will radiate positive thoughts all day and night back out to the conscious mind. But if you allow negativity and bad thoughts to penetrate this powerful part of your mind, a cloud-like barrier will block all positive impulses from radiating forth from the subconscious, and they will never be realized by your conscious.

What an incentive to begin today. Write down your affirmation statements, and post them all over your home and workplace until they becomes habit and memorized. Tell everyone who asks about them what they are and represent, and do so in a very enthusiastic way.

Habits

Habits are made and broken many times over in the course of a lifetime. It is said that "we are creatures of habit." Drinking, smoking, drugs, overeating, and sexual dysfunction are all bad habits if done to excess. Many lives have been ruined due to bad habits. Many good families have been torn apart and destroyed due to habits such as drinking, drugging, stealing, physical abuse, and so on.

You may remember the story of Og Mandino, who ruined his marriage through his drinking, and then almost took his own life. But Og turned his life around—so much so that he became the best-read self-help author of all time. Og broke his bad habits and turned his life around with self-help books.

Habit is defined, in the Merriam-Webster dictionary, as "an acquired mode of behavior that has become nearly or completely involuntary." We each have some bad habits. Many of us have also developed some good habits.

It is important to realize that a new habit is formed in approximately twenty days. Twenty is something of a "magic number" of days to form a new habit or to break an undesirable one. Twenty consecutive days of non-smoking might well enable a smoker to stop, potentially for good.

So, if we know that something practiced for twenty consecutive days will likely form a habit in the brain, then we can make some major improvements in life. If we begin saying self-help affirmation statements numerous times and in the same way each day, after twenty days they will have become engrained in our subconscious mind and our life will change.

The beginning of a habit is like an invisible thread, but every time we repeat the act, we strengthen the strand, add to it another filament, until it becomes a great cable and binds us irrevocably in thought and act.

—Orison Swett Marden (1850-1924),
American writer and founder of *Success* magazine

In Joseph Murphy's book, *Putting the Power of Your Subconscious Mind to Work*, he delves into the acceptance of both negative and positive thoughts by your subconscious. He writes:

"Your subconscious mind is like the soil, which accepts any kind of idea—good or bad...Negative, destructive thoughts continue to work negatively in your subconscious mind and in due time will evolve into actions that correspond with them...If you consciously assume something to be true, even though it may be false, your subconscious mind will accept it as true and proceed to bring about results that must necessarily follow if it were true."

Someone may want to run in the New York City Marathon, even though he never ran a marathon before. I would suggest the following: First, go to the Internet and print out all the statistics for the last race. Also print a registration form. Then print out a photo of someone finishing the race. Post copies of the stats and photo at work and home and near your home computer. Then print out a banner that reads, "NYC MARATHON" with your name added on it and post it somewhere, such as your bedroom. Then formulate a training schedule and purchase new running shoes. Also, research online for a training regimen to follow. Next, tell everyone you know about your intentions. Next, repeat the following self-suggestion statement every day at least five times: "I will be prepared to race the New York City Marathon, and will feel exhilarated when I finish!"

For anything worth having, one must pay the price; and the price is always work, patience, love, self-sacrifice.

—**John Burroughs** (1837-1921), American essayist and naturalist

We Are Each Born into This World Destined for Greatness!

Clarence Crane invented the still-popular LifeSavers candy. During the hot summer of 1913, Clarence, a chocolate-candy manufacturer, discovered the hard candy that wouldn't melt like the chocolates he had been trying to ship.

He was losing orders for his chocolates because of the unusually hot summer. So, to retain his customers, he came up with the non-melting alternative to chocolate. He began making his candies on a machine that had been used for making medicine pills, giving the LifeSavers that unique hole in the middle. They were an instant success.

Chapter Nineteen

Never—Ever—Give Up

When you get into a tight place and everything goes against you, till it seems as though you could not hold on a minute longer, never give up then, for that is just the place and time that the tide will turn.

—Harriet Beecher Stowe (1811-1896), Author

I am always inspired by centenarians—those special people who, against all odds, live to or even past the age of one hundred. I am in awe of them when I see or hear them interviewed and find they still possess a sharp memory, though their body may be broken down.

After all, I believe that we all are minds that carry along a body for life, but in reality, it is our mind that carries us to the end. Some such people whom I have encountered have such vivid memories that go all the way back to their early childhood!

One day I clipped an obituary of a gentleman who passed after reaching the age of 112. The man, an African-American, had lived through both World Wars, the landing of man on the moon, and the election of the first black president, whom he himself had been able to vote for.

As I studied the obituary, I saw that the man was born in 1896 during times of discrimination and was refused entry into the U.S. Army when he tried to apply. I marveled at how this man far surpassed so many others born in the same year, when the average life expectancy of the times was about 42. Amid all the sickness in those days, this man seemed to sidestep it, as if tiptoeing through a minefield. To live to the age of 112 years and 98 days, a person would have lived over 41,000 days. I bet there are many factors involved in longevity, including luck, heredity, faith, lifestyle, and, most important, attitude. Without the right attitude and zest for life, one would be hard-pressed to outlive so many others.

Never give up! That is the inner attitude of the body and mind of anyone who can live for 41,000 days.

The Will to Succeed

What does it take to make it? What does it really take? Let me drop this one on you. In order to be successful, you must be willing to do things today that others won't do in order to have the things tomorrow others won't have.

—**Les Brown** (b. 1945), Motivational speaker

The greatest successes in history had to fight their way to the top. There are no easy roads to riches; the roads are filled with land mines that keep exploding. The real winners know how to keep moving forward and never, ever look back at past mistakes or the many land mines that detonated along the way.

Fred Astaire was probably the best dancer of his time, as well as a movie star who starred in many wonderful musicals and films. But after his first screen test in 1933, the memo from the director of testing at MGM reported, "Can't act. Can't sing. Slightly bald. Can dance a little." Astaire kept that memo over the fireplace in his Beverly Hills home. He once said, "When you're experimenting, you have to try so many things before you choose what you want that you may go days getting nothing but exhaustion. And here is the reward for perseverance: The higher up you go, the more mistakes you are allowed."

Chester Carlson, the inventor of the Xerox machine in 1940, received a rejection letter that read as follows: "Who the hell wants to copy a document on plain paper???" Twenty other companies rejected the idea as "useless." Today, Xerox has revenues each year of about $1 billion.

In 1853, Chef George Crum was cooking at a restaurant in a resort in Saratoga Springs, New York, when a patron returned an order of French fries. The patron complained that the potatoes were too thick. So, to rile up the patron, Crum sliced the potatoes paper-thin and sent the dish back out to the patron. It was a hit—the invention of the potato chip! Everyone soon began ordering them. Crum started his own restaurant shortly thereafter, and the potato chip went down in history as one of the best-loved snacks ever.

In 1928, Walter Diemer was an accountant at the Fleer Chewing Gum Company in Pennsylvania. He was playing around with new recipes for gum when he invented a new type. The first year "bubble gum" was introduced, over $1.5 million worth sold in the U.S. alone.

Spencer Silver invented a low-tack adhesive while working at 3M in 1968. The company rejected it for use in products. But the real man with perseverance was a co-worker who found a use for the low-tack adhesive. Art Fry, also a 3M employee, needed to keep music sheets from falling off the music stand when he sang at his church on Sundays. So he put some of Silver's adhesive on the back of his song sheets. He soon realized the usefulness of this special product and created the 3M Post-It. At first, 3M rejected the idea as impractical, but they realized, after trials, that it was perfect for all offices. The rest is history.

Authors are almost always rejected when presenting a new book to a publisher. The book *Chicken Soup for the Soul*, by Jack Canfield, was rejected one hundred forty times. It finally was accepted and has sold over eighty million copies.

Stephen King's *Carrie* was rejected thirty times.

John Grisham's first book was rejected by sixteen agents and twelve publishers.

It has been noted that Henry Ford failed and went broke five times before succeeding beyond all expectations.

Have patience with all things, but chiefly have patience with yourself. Do not lose courage in considering your own imperfections, but instantly set about remedying them—every day begin the task anew.

—Saint Francis DeSales (1567-1622),
Roman Catholic Bishop of Geneva

You see a pattern in the truly successful. They persevere, usually against all odds. Their ideas are usually rejected as foolish, unworkable, not marketable, or just plain junk. How difficult it must be to believe so strongly in an idea that many others knock. And usually the one knocking the unique new idea is a person in power.

How many innovators gave up too soon with their ideas, only to see someone else make slight modifications and receive all the credit and revenues?

The Mindset to Succeed

We have discussed the immigrant's desire to succeed in America. The word *failure* does not enter the immigrant's mind, as they want more than anything else to make it in America. After all, America has long been recognized as "The Land of Opportunity."

Immigrants understand that all you need to do is work very hard and you will make it in America. What a disgrace it would be for an immigrant to travel back to his own country as a failure. There have been and still are immigrants who become millionaires in our country. I have researched just a handful to make a point. The following immigrants are from all walks of life and have become very successful in America:

Charles Atlas immigrated from Italy in 1903 and became known as a bodybuilder and a business executive.

Irving Berlin immigrated from Russia in 1893 and became known as a famous music composer.

Samuel Goldwyn immigrated from Poland in 1896 and became known as a movie mogul.

Bob Hope immigrated from England in 1908 and became known as one of the most famous comedians and entertainers in history.

Sigmund Freud immigrated from Vienna in 1909 and became known as a psychiatry pioneer.

Charlie Chaplin immigrated from England in 1912 and became known as one of the finest comedy actors.

Albert Einstein immigrated from Germany in 1921 and became known as the finest physicist innovator.

Stan Laurel immigrated from England in 1912 and became known as a great comedic actor.

Levi Strauss immigrated from Bavaria in 1847 and became known for being the founder of the Levi Strauss jeans empire.

Andrew Carnegie immigrated from Scotland in 1848 and became known as a famous industrialist and philanthropist.

America is known as the melting pot of the world. Many of the immigrants of the past had to pass through Ellis Island in New York and have helped to change our world.

The most difficult thing is the decision to act; the rest is merely tenacity. The fears are paper tigers. You can do anything you decide to do.

   —Amelia Earhart (1897-1937?), American aviation pioneer

We know that most immigrants who enter our country possess that "magic" mindset, that powerful, burning desire deeply imbedded in their subconscious mind that says, "I must succeed; I will succeed in America. My family will be very proud of me!"

We each can develop that magic burning desire to succeed.

Let's assume for a minute that you received a call from Donald Trump. He asked you to appear on a new television show he had just started called *Million Dollar Challenge.* The deal is this: Trump will put up one million tax-free dollars in your attorney's escrow account. The money will be awarded to you in ten years, but only if you are successful in completing an assignment. The assignment is this: You must attend college and study for and pass the licensing exam to become a doctor, dentist, chiropractor, or veterinarian. The choice is yours. All your school and living expenses would be paid.

If you pass, the one million tax-free dollars will be released to you immediately. But you must pass the exam on the first try. If you fail, the money will be donated to charity.

Now, the all-important question is this: Will you accept the assignment? You have nothing to lose. The next question is this: Out of every one hundred individuals offered this unique and lucrative deal, how many will succeed?

I would venture to guess over 90 percent would complete the assignment and pass on their first try, capturing the million-dollar payoff. Would your mindset be similar to the immigrant entering our country with fantastic dreams and goals? You bet it would.

You would be so pumped up every waking morning. You would visualize the one million tax-free dollars. In fact, over the ten years, you would envision the finish line over one million times. I would feel sorry for anyone who stood in your way, tried to talk you out of the challenge, or was just being downright negative about all the work ahead of you.

Next question: Would you go for the full eight-year physician degree, or opt for a lesser, easier college degree that would have a higher likelihood of passing successfully? That, of course, would be your choice. But some would go the full distance and become a physician. Many, though, would choose the easier, higher passing-percentage degree, thus guaranteeing the tax-free $1 million payoff.

Again, it's only mindset. It is properly programming your mind to accept a goal and work until it has been successfully achieved.

Maybe you have moved in the past. When we prepare to change our residence, we first program this data, the entire moving process, into our mind. Over the course of weeks, our subconscious mind becomes prepared for and accepts the monumental task of moving—packing, changing utilities, painting, cleaning, unpacking, arranging, and so on.

It is a tremendous undertaking, but the energy level is there through the entire project. The subconscious prepares and constantly sends out signals of motivation and assurance of the eventual completion of the entire moving process, convincing the conscious mind on a regular basis that there is much farther to go to the finish line, but that it *can* be reached. This is, I believe, what energizes and pushes the body onward to accomplish a great deal of work—to actually out-perform the unmotivated mind and body. In other words, if we were told that in five minutes we needed to begin working and work for eighteen hours straight on a given project, and if that project were of a non-emergency nature, we might not be able to accomplish the task. But if we were to accomplish it, we would be much more exhausted than the highly-motivated and pre-programmed person who is moving and needs to work eighteen hours straight.

On the other hand, if we were told that our relative or best friend had been hurt in a fire and that, starting in five minutes, his house needed to be cleaned up, fixed, painted, decorated, etc., over an eighteen-hour period, we no doubt would be able to pull it off. The subconscious mind would be programmed so strongly within a few minutes' time as to the urgency of the situation and the need for immediate action and compassion. This alone would be enough to carry us to the finish line.

So, what is it that you want to get all fired up about? Is it working a second job to save up for a down payment for a new home or car? Is it sending your children to college or camp, or is it something else? Do you want to change jobs so badly, but must first complete certain requirements that you have previously ignored? Do you want to save up to have enough to get married? See how I keep challenging you to look deep into your heart for that special goal?

Whatever it is, you can now see the mindset needed to accomplish near-miracles.

See It Through

When you're up against a trouble,
Meet it squarely, face to face;
Lift your chin and set your shoulders,

Plant your feet and take a brace.
When it's vain to try to dodge it,

Do the best that you can do;
You may fail, but you may conquer,

See it through!
Black may be the clouds about you

And your future may seem grim,
But don't let your nerve desert you;

Keep yourself in fighting trim.
If the worst is bound to happen,

Spite of all that you can do,
Running from it will not save you,

See it through!
Even hope may seem but futile,

When with troubles you're beset,
But remember you are facing

Just what other men have met.
You may fail, but fall still fighting;

Don't give up, whate'er you do;
Eyes front, head high to the finish,

See it through!

—**Edgar Guest** (1881-1959), American poet

Plan to Become a Person of Belief

Any worthwhile achievement needs special planning and commitment. Nothing monumental ever happens by just winging it. Successful people plan on being successful. So, why not write down, in detail, notes to help you believe greater in yourself:

1. Take stock of yourself, where you are currently.
2. Take a full accounting of your health at this moment. Are you ill or do you have conditions that affect your daily living?
3. Believe that what you truly desire to accomplish in life is worthwhile. Write out exactly why your goal is so important to you.
4. Plan out how you can believe more deeply in your desired goals. What changes will you make, starting today, to achieve this goal? Write them out. Post your statement of goals everywhere in plain sight. Remember, "Out of sight, out of mind!"
5. Create a positive buffer-shield, a barrier which negative thoughts and negative people cannot penetrate.

6. Replace all negative words with positive words. Write these words down and post them in places where you will see them each day.

7. Custom-make your own positive self-suggestion statements. Use these affirmations throughout your day, every day.

8. Each and every day, find a quiet place, and for ten minutes do the following: Sitting quietly, undisturbed, close your eyes. Next, breathing only through your nose, draw in a deep, slow breath for five full seconds. Then exhale, again through your nose, but as you slowly exhale for ten seconds, say the following:

> "I let out all the stress from my body!"
> "I release all fear of success!"
> "I will be successful!"
> "I was born for greatness!"

We Are Each Born into This World Destined for Greatness!

Jack Taylor, born in 1923, achieved greatness by founding the highly successful Enterprise Rent-A-Car business. Taylor dropped out of Washington University and served in the Navy as a fighter pilot aboard the USS *Enterprise* during World War II. He later became a sales manager for a Cadillac dealership. Sometime after that, he took a 50 percent cut in salary to start a company that provided people with replacement cars while their vehicle was being repaired. And in the 1970s, the business took off big-time. Enterprise revenues today exceed $10 billion. Taylor has been ranked the eighteenth-richest American, with a net worth of $9.5 billion.

Chapter Twenty

Perseverance: The Difference Winners Always Practice

When faced with a mountain, I will not quit! I will keep on striving until I climb over, find a pass through, tunnel underneath, or simply stay and turn the mountain into a goldmine, with God's help!

—Friedrich von Schiller (1759-1805),
German poet, philosopher, historian and playwright

For over thirty years, I have studied the truly successful—the pioneers, the inventors, the millionaires. I truly admire Ford, Edison, Napoleon Hill, Lincoln, Og Mandino, and so many others.

The common denominator I have found in all the great achievers is *perseverance*. Nothing stands in the way of a great achiever. All roadblocks are somehow moved away. No matter how down they are, how beaten they may appear to be, they suddenly rise up to the challenge and come out victorious.

Champions aren't made in the gyms. Champions are made from something they have deep inside them—a desire, a dream, a vision.

—Muhammad Ali (b. 1942), American professional boxer, World Heavyweight Champion, 1960 Summer Olympics gold medalist

Let's look at some outstanding people who have achieved greatness. It's not because they were superhuman, but simply because they pursued their dreams, undeterred, till the end.

Can you imagine being the first surgeon to attempt a human organ transplant? What tremendous skepticism and criticism there must have been each time a transplant was attempted on a new organ!

The first successful organ transplant was done over fifty years ago by Dr. Joseph Murray. No one had ever performed a successful transplant on a human being before. All earlier attempts—more than thirty of them!—had failed. Critics accused Dr. Murray of playing God. There was more rejection than support for the doctor. And how about the doctor's own confidence level? Dr. Murray had everything going against him. And keep in mind, medical technology then was nowhere as advanced as it is today. Yet, in 1954, Dr. Murray successfully performed a breakthrough kidney transplant on a 23-year-old man. The man lived eight years, which at the time was remarkable.

Dr. Christian Barnard created a medical breakthrough in 1967 with the first successful heart transplant. Barnard led a thirty-member surgical team in the first transplant of its kind. The doctor once said, "It is infinitely better to transplant a heart than to bury it so it can be devoured by worms." Dr. Barnard prepared for years in advance in order to perform that first heart transplant inside a human. He even performed transplant operations on animals first. What tremendous conviction the doctor had! What a positive mindset he must have had at the time of the operation!

In the late sixties, Federal Express founder Frederick W. Smith developed his idea of overnight delivery service. The notion was initially frowned upon, but after years of believing in his idea, he convinced Wall Street investors. Fed Ex started out with eight planes and covered approximately forty cities. Then it caught on big-time, turning into a company worth more than $35 billion.

J. K. Rowling is reported to be the second richest female entertainer in the world, behind Oprah Winfrey. Everyone knows Rowling as the author of the Harry Potter series, later connected to all the movies. What people didn't know until she became more famous is that Rowling was poor, living on public assistance. Her life was upside down amid a messy divorce and her mother dying. Her first Harry Potter novel in 1995 was rejected by twelve different publishers. She was told by one publisher to go out and find a day job. But now, the Harry Potter empire she built is valued at around $15 billion. Someone with less conviction would easily have given up. It goes to show you that if you truly believe in yourself and work on in spite of all the negatives, you just could become another J. K. Rowling.

Others have also forged ahead despite ridicule and skepticism, and in so doing have made the world a better place. The following are some quotes that were once spoken in opposition to the progress we have all enjoyed. Regarding space travel:

To place a man in a multi-stage rocket and project him into the controlling gravitational field of the moon where the passengers can make scientific observations, perhaps land alive, and then return to earth—all that constitutes a wild dream worthy of Jules Verne. I am bold enough to say that such a manmade voyage will never occur regardless of all future advances.

—Lee De Forest (1873-1961),
American radio pioneer and inventor of the vacuum tube

And only eighteen months prior to the Wright brothers' successful flight at Kitty Hawk, the following was said concerning the notion of an airplane:

Flight by machines heavier than air is unpractical and insignificant, if not utterly impossible.

—Simon Newcomb (1835-1909)
Canadian-American astronomer and mathematician

Steve Jobs was only in his twenties when he co-founded Apple Computers on April 1, 1976, along with Steve Wozniak. The two were high school dropouts with a dream and a knack for computers. Together they built an empire and employed several thousand people.

In a commencement speech he gave at Stanford University in 2005, Jobs put it all in a nutshell when he said, "Your time is limited, so don't waste it living someone else's life. Don't be trapped by dogma—which is living with the results of other people's thinking. Don't let the noise of others' opinions drown out your own inner voice. And most important, have the courage to follow your heart and intuition. They somehow already know what you truly want to become. Everything else is secondary."

We have discussed motivation, planting thoughts and dreams into your subconscious mind, and shielding negative thoughts from your inner mind. Allow me to use something mundane to demonstrate the wisdom of these practices.

Just a few minutes ago, while putting out the Sunday evening garbage for Monday pick-up, I wrote an entire song. You see, deep in my subconscious I have etched the desire to write songs, though I don't play an instrument. I have, on occasion, even written two songs in a day. This evening, a couple of words in my mind spurred an entire song. I quickly grabbed my trusty mini-cassette recorder and sang the new creation into it. In five minutes flat I recorded perhaps the best song I have ever written. To me it sounded that good! (although now I cannot recall any of it, which is why I record them immediately!).

Here is my point: The subconscious mind will, when least expected, come forth with great ideas and answers to your most troubling questions. This is why, just as I keep my mini-recorder handy, I also keep a pen and paper on my nightstand. I have on many occasions in the middle of the night come up with ideas for books and business. The subconscious is that powerful. Don't fight the urge to try it out. You will be amazed. There have been many inventors who have said that some of their best ideas come in the middle of the night.

A Driving Force

Lance Armstrong has within him a positive driving force. He was a professional road-racing cyclist when, in 1996, at age 25, he was diagnosed with testicular cancer. If that weren't enough, the cancer metastasized to his brain and lungs. His cancer treatments included testicular and brain surgery, as well as extensive chemotherapy. Armstrong's prognosis was poor. But not only did he beat the cancer; he went on to win the Tour de France for a record seven consecutive years. No one had ever won such a grueling bike race seven years in a row! In 2009, after taking a few years off, Armstrong returned to racing. And at age 38, he wound up finishing third. Clearly, Armstrong has the heart of a champion and the drive to succeed in whatever he undertakes.

The greatest achievement was at first and for a time a dream. The oak sleeps in the acorn, the bird waits in the egg, and in the highest vision of the soul a waking angel stirs. Dreams are the seedlings of realities.

—James Allen (1864-1912), British author

In James Allen's self-help masterpiece book *As a Man Thinketh*, published in 1904, he writes of the inner mind: "Just as a gardener cultivates his plot, keeping it free from weeds, and growing the flowers and fruits which he requires, so may a man tend the garden of his mind, weeding out all the wrong, useless, and impure thoughts, and cultivating toward perfection the flowers and fruits of right, useful, and pure thoughts. By pursuing this process, a man sooner or later discovers that he is the master-gardener of his soul, the director of his life. He also reveals, within himself, the flaws of thought, and understands, with ever-increasing accuracy, how the thought-forces and mind-elements operate in the shaping of character, circumstances, and destiny."

James Allen was "right on" with his writings in 1904 and even earlier. So I wanted to show you what life was like in 1904. Here is a snapshot:

The Year 1904

The average life expectancy was forty-seven. Only 14 percent of homes had a bathtub. Eight percent had a telephone. There were only eight thousand cars in the U.S. Ninety-five percent of all births took place in the home. Only 6 percent of all Americans graduated from high school. Look how far we have advanced! Medical technology now saves most of the lives that would have been lost in 1904. You really are alive at the best time ever in America. We have it all! You have a better opportunity to become a success today than in any year in the past.

Even James Allen, the brilliant writer and thinker of his day, only lived to age forty-eight. We are much more energetic and healthy at all ages today than back then. Our only excuse for not becoming successful today is in the limits of our thinking and our pure driving force.

So, separate yourself from the average person today. Cultivate your inner mind, stretch your thinking, work to convince your mind to accept what you want to accomplish.

There is absolutely nothing wrong with being average. The average person works hard and helps keep this country running. But why not stand out from the crowd? Why not become a leader and an innovator—someone who can change the world?

Change is the end result of all true learning. Change involves three things: First, a dissatisfaction with self—a felt void or need; second, a decision to change to fill the void or need; and third, a conscious dedication to the process of growth and change—the willful act of making the change, doing something.

—**Leo Buscaglia** (1924-1998), Author and motivational speaker

We Are Each Born into This World Destined for Greatness!

Donald Trump, a real estate developer and mogul, was born on June 14, 1946, in Queens, New York, the fourth of five children. Donald made his own way after attending Wharton Business School and working with his father, Fred, for five years. Trump clearly took after his father, who was himself a wealthy real estate developer. The younger Trump slowly became one of Manhattan's real estate moguls. He now produces his own television show, and *Forbes* has him ranked among the 488 wealthiest billionaires in the world. Trump is clearly a driven individual, a go-getter who maintains a positive attitude.

Chapter Twenty-One

The Greatest Living Miracle in the World

Twenty years from now, you will be more disappointed by the things you did not do than by the things you did do. So throw off the bowlines. Sail away from the safe harbor. Catch the trade winds in your sails. Explore. Dream. Discover.

—**Mark Twain** (1835-1910),American author and humorist

I have always been a very confident individual. There are few things I don't believe I can accomplish if I set my mind to them. A few years ago, I took some of my novels and adapted them for motion pictures. I wrote or co-wrote the movie scripts and then set out to find backers to make the films.

Well, a few years, and thousands of dollars, later—money I invested or got swindled out of—the result is that I realize the motion picture industry is a very tough field to break into and that there are many con artists. But in the end, I don't regret trying to get my scripts made into films. If I had not attempted to make them into films, I would have always regretted not trying at all. In the end, I am still happy because I have three movie scripts written.

You are the greatest living miracle in the world! No one else in the world has your exact eyes, hair, fingerprints, personality, or DNA. The odds of your being born into the specific person and personality you are have been estimated at one in 225 billion. You are the most unique person in the world.

By the age of seventy, the average human heart will have beaten two-and-a-half billion times. Your heart pumps over fifty-seven thousand gallons of blood every month. The heart is an amazing organ! There are people alive today who have lived 115 years—you do the math. Suffice it to say that we are each a phenomenal working mechanism that still cannot be duplicated.

No matter what our financial status at this particular moment, whether we have fifty cents to our name or $50 million, each one of us is an equally great miracle in the world.

We all may say we are special, but do you believe it with all your heart?

You are the greatest living miracle in the world. Once you realize this, you will begin to appreciate just how very special you really are. Your eyes, if we could place value on them alone, are worth at least a billion dollars to a person who can't see. Your hearing ability and your ability to stand up and walk are awesome blessings.

The question is, are you *acting* like the greatest living miracle in the world? Each of us was created by God. A true miracle took place in those nine months of gestation in order for you to be born. Now think about the following question very carefully:

If God presented Himself to you right now, and He just stared at you without saying a word, just studying you for a few precious seconds, would you feel proud about your accomplishments thus far in life? Would you feel that you have used the miracle of your life to the best of your ability, or would you feel that you have cheated God, slightly or drastically, in return for the miracle He allowed to be performed through your birth?

What if, just possibly, we do live on in a special afterlife? What if we are left to reflect upon our lives in minute detail, second after second, and we must ponder this life for eternity? I don't know about you, but I already want to accomplish much more. You see, I do believe there is an afterlife. I also believe that all your relatives, friends, and acquaintances who have passed on to this afterlife are observing you, rooting for you, and anxiously waiting for you to achieve greatness.

Here is a small sample of another affirmation I repeat to myself every day without modification:

"God loves me unconditionally. He watches over me every single minute of every day, and He roots for me in all that I do. All He asks is that I remain honorable. Jesus and His mother Mary watch over me every single minute of every day, and they root for me in all that I do. All they ask is that I remain honorable. All the relatives, friends, neighbors, and acquaintances who have passed on watch over me every single minute of every day, and they root for me in all that I do. All they ask is that I remain honorable..."

The affirmation goes on for another three minutes. Its sequence has never changed. You see, it serves as a daily reminder that my life is an important asset that must not be wasted. And just possibly, if I am being observed by my grandfather, my grandmother, my father who raised me, and my uncles who loved me, I will not let them or myself down.

Og Mandino, in his fabulous book *The Greatest Salesman in the World*, said it best:

I will persist until I succeed. I was not delivered into this world in defeat, nor does failure course in my veins. I am not a sheep waiting to be prodded by my Shepherd. I am a lion and I refuse to talk, to walk, to sleep with the sheep. The slaughterhouse of failure is not my destiny. I will persist until I succeed.

With Vision and Dreams You Can Succeed

Who would ever think that putting rivets onto pants would be accepted by consumers?

Levi Strauss and his partner Jacob Davis believed they had something revolutionary when they invented the first blue jeans in 1873. They had come up with the idea of placing rivets at the points of strain on workers' pants. They put rivets at the pocket corners and the base of the fly, and used special material for strength. What a brilliant idea! But we know that new, revolutionary ideas are not always well received at first.

Well, as they say, the rest is history. In the case of the Levi Strauss jeans, they were a hit! Workers loved them, and soon everyone was wearing the very durable pants that could outlast all other such products.

Imagine a product invented in 1873 and whose basic concept is still used all these years later. Think outside the box. Those who do so usually achieve greatness, as Levi Strauss and Jacob Davis did.

In 1897, Felix Hoffmann, a German chemist, invented a new compound of acetylsalicylic acid, which came to be known as aspirin. Hoffmann was trying to come up with something to alleviate his father's arthritis. Today, aspirin is used to save millions of lives. It is basically the same as it was when it proved useful in 1897. You see, Hoffmann did research into another chemist's creation from 1832 and discovered that the earlier chemist's compound could be effective in many areas; in effect, Hoffmann rediscovered it. Today, all these years later, it is understood that aspirin can guard against heart attacks and, if taken immediately by someone experiencing a heart attack, often saves the victim's life.

Working under Pressure Can Be Useful

In 1849, Walter Hunt was under pressure to find a way to pay back a $15 debt. Knowledgeable about how to invent things, he set out to solve his problem.

Hunt took a piece of wire made of brass, about eighteen inches in length, coiled the center of it, and shielded one end, making the very first safety pin. Hunt took out a patent, sold off the rights for $400, and paid back his debt to his friend. The safety pin is still in use today—another brilliant idea from someone under pressure to come up with a way to solve an immediate problem.

Could this be an example of a man who needed an answer turning his problem over to his subconscious mind? It sounds like a perfect example to me. I have used this method many times. Before falling off to sleep, I consciously ask my subconscious mind to come up with new ideas for a book I am working on. One night recently, at two o'clock and again at three o'clock, I was awakened with ideas that would not allow me to go right back to sleep. So I reached for paper and pen, always kept on my nightstand, and wrote out my thoughts there, in the total darkness. Not until the morning light did I realize I had found the answers to some questions I had been stuck on in my writing for a couple of weeks.

In the early 1940s, Swiss inventor George de Mestral was hit with an idea. Upon returning from walking his dog, he noticed cockleburs attached to the dog's coat and on his own pants. His curiosity compelled him to study the burrs under a microscope. It was the beginning thought which led to the invention known now as Velcro.

Those who have attained things worth having in this world have worked while others idled, have persevered when others gave up in despair, have practiced early in life the valuable habits of self-denial, industry, and singleness of purpose. As a result, they enjoy in later life the success so often erroneously attributed to good luck!

    —Grenville Kleiser (1868-1935), North American author

Is Your Attitude Contagious?

Are you contagious? You bet you are! We are each very contagious in our attitude. Notice how a dog or a child studies another's eyes, looking for fear, threat, or approval. Our eyes and faces tell a story like the words of a book. Because of that, you are highly contagious.

Whatever you are thinking, feeling, experiencing at a particular moment is transmitted to everyone around you, which makes it crucial that you be careful of what you project to the world. You can project negativity, or you can project a positive attitude. Imagine what a difference it could make if you infected another person with a positive attitude and then *that* person also became contagious and infected someone else!

If it is to be, it must begin with me.

**We Are Each Born into This
World Destined for Greatness!**

Edwin Beard Budding invented the first lawn mower in 1830. Budding was an engineer from England. His new lawn mower consisted of a set of blades in a cylinder on two wheels. As the mower was pushed, the cylinder would rotate, and the blades trimmed the grass. The new lawn mower was patented in August 1830. A brilliant idea, way ahead of its time. Before Budding's lawn mower, animals were allowed to graze the grass to keep it trimmed!

Chapter Twenty-Two

You Can Become Resilient, Like the Human Body

Perseverance is absolutely essential, not just to produce all those words, but to survive rejection and criticism. However, the utter joy of seeing a book you wrote sitting in a bookshelf is a prize worth striving for.

—**J. K. Rowling** (b. 1965), British author of the "Harry Potter" series

The human body is very resilient. In fact, the body is constantly striving to stay alive, without our being privy on a conscious level to all the behind-the-scenes activities. The brain, like a huge manufacturing plant, runs our body, most often without our awareness.

That is precisely why the thoughts we feed our brains are so important. Our brains can make us sick, kill us off, or heal the most dreaded disease. It is a chemical manufacturing plant that mixes many thousands of recipes of chemicals that science still doesn't fully understand. But this much is for certain—you can live healthier by thinking positive thoughts and eliminating most of the stress.

We cut our nails and our hair, and they quickly regrow. We injure ourselves by cutting our finger or breaking a bone, and the body fixes itself. The brain quickly concocts the precise mixture of chemicals to race to the site of trauma, the cut or broken bone, and the mending process begins.

The body also is in a constant state of survival. There are so many bacteria, viruses, parasites, and so forth always trying to overtake our body, so it is continually working to maintain its healthy balance. Don't ever think that your body is not in battle twenty-four hours a day, every day. Most bodies are victorious for many years. Sometimes the battle ends too soon in early death for various reasons. But you can play a huge role in keeping your body and, more important, your mind in tip-top shape.

Our body is a work of art, a priceless masterpiece that will never, ever be duplicated. For all the money in the world we could never build a machine such as our body-and-mind combination.

Our lives are similar in nature to our bodies. Each and every day we are threatened in many ways. Our jobs are never guaranteed. Our lives are not guaranteed from day to day. We walk the busy streets, drive in unpredictable cars and on highways that can be hazardous. Yet, most of us survive, thrive, and go on each and every new day.

In August 2010, we were shocked when thirty-three miners were suddenly trapped in a century-old gold and copper mine in Chile.

Sixty-nine days after a rock collapse sealed the San Jose Mine, all thirty-three men were rescued in good health.

It was a miracle, for sure. All odds were stacked against the miners surviving at all. Approximately 700,000 tons of rock had collapsed in the mine. For seventeen days, in darkness and with almost no food or liquids, the miners wondered if anyone would ever find them.

The miners rationed the few supplies they had one-half mile below the surface, praying someone would be able to locate their small area of refuge. They allowed themselves only two teaspoonfuls of tuna every other day, a sip of milk, and a bite of a cracker. They learned to extract water from the rocks that surrounded them.

The miners managed to conserve the minimal food and air. When the rescuers finally bored a correct hole into their area some seventeen days after the collapse, it was estimated that the miners would have had only twenty-four hours of air remaining in their 600-square-foot survival area.

They remained buried for over fifty-two more days, until a larger hole could be carefully bored, just wide enough for a rescue capsule on a pulley to be slowly and meticulously lowered to raise each one to safety.

What a tremendous will to live and what faith the miners had! When life is in jeopardy, most people will do and endure anything in order to survive. And the non-stop efforts from above on the part of rescuers who would not stop working for sixty-nine days until the miners were all saved, was inspiring to watch.

What I observed as I watched it all unfold was the elation each miner showed as soon as they emerged from that hole. It was an intense appreciation for life that they had once again been blessed with as soon as they were safe. We all could learn an important lesson from these miners. Every day we are given is a true gift from above. We must not squander our days away, not when we realize that some people with no days left would gladly use our day to the utmost.

Life is a crapshoot of sorts, in which anything can happen. Yet, for the most part, we maintain the positive outlook that everything will be fine. We don't think of all the risky possibilities we are faced with every single day. We believe that it will all take care of itself and that we will return home safely each night to our families.

We must begin to treat our dreams and long-term goals the same way. We must always anticipate success, and never dwell on the possibility of failure. We must act as if we were inside our own body, the manufacturing plant of our brain, where nothing is allowed to take control, where the brain constantly adjusts, second by second, for the successful running of the human body it controls.

We were born to succeed! Your body was born to live, not die—to overcome all obstacles. Allow only positive thoughts to enter and control your mind and body.

Where We Have Been

The human mind has been evolving, just as the human body has, over thousands of years, beginning with the caveman trying everything for the first time. But look at how we have evolved and thrived over all those years! Medical technology has allowed many people to surpass one hundred years of age, and many very active centenarians have all their senses about them.

The human brain has taken us from creating fire to cooking a meal over a campsite to inventing and flying a space shuttle so advanced that it boggles the mind. There are 1,607,185 pounds of freezing fuel powering the rocket that blasts the space shuttle off from earth.

How amazing is it that man on earth can send a rocket ship from earth all the way to Mars and have it come safely back to the earth? Look at how far we have advanced to reach these technologically rich days! We enjoy all these latest advances and conveniences of the present day, making our lives so much easier and more productive. Every one of those thirty-three miners trapped in Chile would have perished just ten years earlier. But today we have advanced to a point where they were miraculously saved.

Do we not owe it to society and ourselves to operate like we are in these advanced technological days? Should we not be expected in these times to excel farther than our forefathers and foremothers? We will shortchange ourselves unless we stretch farther, give back more, produce much more than those who preceded us.

I make a special attempt to always strive for more. It is too easy to become satisfied with mediocre results that others admire. We know we can accomplish so much more. We know we are well equipped to achieve far bigger and grander results. Let us never ever be satisfied— not if we know we have not given it our all-out effort. Take note of the great achievers of our past. We can learn to be more aggressive and more confident in ourselves just by studying these great people:

Earle Dickson invented the Band-Aid to help his wife's fingers that kept on getting cuts. In 1921, he invented a piece of tape with the gauze already attached to it. Johnson & Johnson decided to manufacture the new Band-Aid. It was a hit.

In 1837, Samuel Morse changed the world when, in collaboration with Alfred Vail, he created a new form of secret communication— the Morse code. It changed the way the military exchanged interior communication. It was and still is a brilliant, well thought-out invention.

I would not sit waiting for some value tomorrow, nor for something to happen. One could wait a lifetime...I would make something happen.

—Louis L'Amour (1908-1988),
American author, known as "America's Storyteller"

We Are Each Born into This World Destined for Greatness!

Ralph Lauren grew up in the Bronx, New York. His father was a Jewish house painter. Ralph dropped out of City College of New York after just two years. He then worked as a salesman at Brooks Brothers stores. He started a necktie business, created the Polo label, and went on to become one of the most famous fashion designers in the world. Today he is worth a few billion dollars. What is most interesting is that Ralph Lauren never attended fashion school.

People ask how a Jewish kid from the Bronx does preppy clothes. Does it have to do with class and money? It has to do with dreams.

—Ralph Lauren (b. 1939), American fashion designer

Chapter Twenty-Three

The Immense Power of the Mind

If you are not willing to risk, you cannot grow; if you cannot grow, you cannot become your best; if you cannot become your best, you cannot become happy; and if you cannot become happy ... what else is there?

—**Les Brown** (b. 1945), Motivational speaker

Studies show that the human mind is powerful beyond all comprehension. The average person uses only a minute capacity of his or her brain. The brilliant minds of the world use perhaps double the capacity of the average person, but still nowhere near what could be used to maximize the mind's immense power. By reading self-improvement books, we stretch the mind's data-storage area we are using and force new areas of the brain to work.

As I've described in earlier chapters, self-talk, or affirmations, are of utmost importance in improving oneself, and in using more of the powerful mind we all possess. Let's look more closely at how such messages work.

Subliminal Messages

The subconscious mind will accept messages fed into it as fact, as long as the messages are received on a consistent basis. This is very important to remember, as it can be done in various forms and can benefit you greatly. One way to tap into the subconscious is through subliminal messages.

What are subliminal messages, and how do they work? A company called Subliminal Power explains it this way: "Subliminal messages are positive affirmations sent directly to the subconscious mind, bypassing the more critical conscious mind. The subconscious then follows these commands to produce powerful and exciting change quicker than anything . . ."

Subliminal messages can work in various forms: video, print, or audio messages. Your subconscious mind absorbs messages that your conscious mind can't read, see, or hear because your subconscious mind can hear beyond the "music" your conscious mind hears, and then absorbs those background messages. Or it sees messages flashed on a computer screen or a movie screen—words that the conscious mind misses.

Hypnosis also works on the subconscious mind. The person hypnotized receives a series of messages while in a state of sleepiness. The subconscious mind accepts these statements as fact and acts upon the messages. This is why people can often lose weight or stop smoking after receiving messages under hypnosis.

Our verbal affirmations can be just as powerful as subliminal messages or hypnosis if we practice them daily by saying the same statements in the same order over and over. Statements said can be similar to these:

"I like myself.

I am good; I am useful.

I will be successful; it's inevitable, because my aggressiveness will lead to my success.

I will work harder and longer and will succeed.

Nothing will stand in my way to achieve my goal."

The Mind Is Like a Sponge

Some of us watch very carefully what we eat and put inside our bodies. I remember being at lunch with some people who were so particular when ordering food that I couldn't help wondering if it really helped them that much. Years later I saw these same individuals and they had gained so much weight that it was apparent they had stopped practicing that diet!

We can draw an analogy, once again, between the body and the brain. I can't help but think about how little most people watch what is absorbed into their brains. If you work at exercising your body, why not exercise your mind with positive affirmations and inspiring books?

Are We Killing Grandpa with Love?

If our minds are like sponges and our subconscious minds accept what is fed to them, are we watching not only what *we* eat but what we feed to others through our verbal communication?

If we so readily absorb what is fed to us subconsciously through hypnosis, subliminal messages, repeated affirmations, and verbal communication, might we sometimes end up believing something false? I say absolutely, YES! If we could continually convince a 75-year-old person that he is fifty-five through messages to his subconscious, he would begin to act as if he were fifty-five years old.

But, on the other hand, are we, in effect, killing Grandpa with love by reminding him continually about his age and about how amazing it is that he has lived so long? Say, for example, that Grandpa is ninety years old and that, because we love him so much, we brag in front of him about his age. Are we not actually doing him harm? Are we convincing him that it is amazing—actually, unexpected, unnatural—that he is still alive because many people never make it to his age? I say YES!

Are we also hurting our children and grandchildren by telling them to watch out for this or that? Or to not do that, or to be careful? "Watch out for that person!" "Don't try that or you might get hurt!" Have we taken God's creation, the child who was created to be a success, and slowly programmed that child to be fearful and stressed out, to be overly careful, to become lazy and spoiled?

So, watch what light you emanate. The light can be positive or negative, uplifting or deflating. Your light will, in fact, be absorbed by all people with whom you come in contact.

A hundred times a day I remind myself that my inner and outer life are based on the labors of other [people] living and dead, and that I must exert myself in order to give in the same measures as I have received and am still receiving.

—**Albert Einstein** (1878-1955), Physicist and philosopher

Many years ago, when I was twenty-one years old, working as a new life insurance agent, and very impressionable, someone told me something profound. An old senior life insurance agent said, "John, you've got the world by the tail! You don't realize it, but you've really got the world by the tail!" From that day forward, I really believed that—I did have the world by the tail. And one of the statements I repeat in my daily affirmations is the same: "I've got the world by the tail!"

We all have the world by the tail. You see, the older agent said it to me as if *he* no longer had the world by the tail, when, in fact, he had everything going for him: He was close to retiring and would receive a couple of pension payments each month for the rest of his life. His wife and he were healthy and could begin traveling. He had a wonderful daughter and a working car, and he loved to paint. But he believed he no longer had the world by the tail. So, after he retired, it was only about a year and a half later that we attended this once-healthy man's wake and funeral.

What are you feeding your mind today, tomorrow, and forever? Do you have the world by the tail? Absolutely!—as long as you believe that you do!

Those Who Think Differently

In the name of the best within you, do not sacrifice this world to those who are its worst. In the name of the values that keep you alive, do not let your vision of man be distorted by the ugly, the cowardly, the mindless in those who have never achieved his title. Do not lose your knowledge that man's proper estate is an upright posture, an intransigent mind, and a step that travels unlimited roads. Do not let your fire go out, spark by irreplaceable spark, in the hopeless swamps of the approximate, the not-quite, the not-yet, the not-at-all. Do not let the hero in your soul perish, in lonely frustration for the life you deserved but have never been able to reach. Check your road and the nature of your battle. The world you desired can be won, it exists, it is real, it is possible, it's yours.

—**Ayn Rand** (1905-1982), Russian-American philosopher and novelist

The Internet giant YouTube was founded by three young men in 2005. Chad Hurley, Steve Chen, and Jawed Karim came up with the angel-funded company from their makeshift office in a garage. Within its first few months, the company was very popular. In the summer of 2006, YouTube was ranked the fifth most popular website. Today over one hundred million video clips are viewed on it every day. In 2007, YouTube was purchased outright by mega-giant Google for $1.7 billion.

Three young men with a dream, a unique idea, and a vision for success are now multimillionaires and set for the rest of their lives.

Twitter is the very popular website where people "tweet" messages of one hundred forty characters or less to each other and their entire network of "followers." Twitter was founded in 2006 by Evan Williams, Jack Dorsey, and Biz Stone. The network is now over seventy-five million members strong, according to *ComputerWorld*, and worth around $1 billion—all because of three normal guys not afraid to take a chance on a brilliant, new idea.

Each of us is born to be a great success. Each of us has all the same equipment at birth—eyes, mouth, ears, legs, arms, and a brain. Why do some excel while others just barely get by? I believe most of it has to do with our own expectations deep within.

I believe that we can step up, step away from, and stand out from the crowd all around us. By implementing ideas learned from self-help books, you can make small changes in your everyday life that will result in huge changes in your long-term success.

In 1906, an Italian economist, Vilfredo Pareto, created a mathematical formula to describe the unequal distribution of wealth in his country. He observed that 20 percent of the people owned 80 percent of the wealth. It has also been said that 20 percent of a person's efforts produce 80 percent of their results.

I take it one step further: I suspect that only roughly 20 percent of the people who read self-help and motivational books such as this one actually change and improve their lives enough to make a real difference and be more successful. My sense is that only a small percentage of people believe they need to change anything in their lives strongly enough to go out of their way to make the changes necessary to improve.

The great revolution in our generation is that of human beings, who by changing the inner attitudes of their minds, can change the outer aspects of their lives.

—**William James** (1842-1910), American philosopher and psychologist

> # We Are Each Born into This
> # World Destined for Greatness!

Richard Desmond, born on December 8, 1951, was living with his mother in a garage apartment after his parents' divorce. He had dropped out of school at the age of fourteen, had become a drummer, and worked in a newspaper classifieds department. But by age twenty-one, after working at another company, he soon owned two record stores. By the next year, Richard had acquired an interest in a publishing company and in 1974 published a magazine called *International Musician and Recording World*. He currently owns dozens of titles—a true "rags to riches" story. In 2009 he was ranked as the forty-fourth richest man in Britain.

Chapter Twenty-Four

The Hourglass of Time

All my possessions for a moment of time.

—**Elizabeth I** (1558-1603), Queen of England

Time is that precious commodity we have all been blessed with. How much time is inside our own personal hourglass no one knows. The ninety-year-old has already been blessed with over 32,870 days.

But here is the problem with that hourglass. Once that personal hourglass is almost empty, there is nothing that person can do. No king, president, billionaire, or peasant has ever been able to add one second of time to his own personal hourglass. Once it's empty, life on earth comes to an end for that individual. The hereafter, as it is often called, and in which many people believe, will then commence.

No, we cannot buy time, but we can manage it and avoid squandering the time we have been blessed with.

Don't say you don't have enough time. You have exactly the same number of hours per day that were given to Helen Keller, Pasteur, Michelangelo, Mother Teresa, Leonardo da Vinci, Thomas Jefferson, and Albert Einstein.

—**H. Jackson Brown, Jr.,** American author

The average person wastes so many hours per week it should be a crime. Did you ever take inventory? I say "inventory" because, as with a shopkeeper, those hours you have been blessed with are yours to cherish.

When you waste them, it is as if they have been stolen from you for good. But you are the real thief of your own wasted time.

Let's take account of time and how it can be maximized. Assuming we get up at seven o'clock each day to go to work, what if we were to get up at 6:45 instead? Those fifteen additional minutes would equal ninety-one hours per year. That time could be spent on exercising, self-development reading, writing, or other self-help training. Do not discount fifteen minutes per day. Fifteen minutes' exercise could mean the difference of several pounds per year and a firmer, trimmer body.

Next, we may take an hour a day to leave work, go out somewhere, and pretty much waste the time on lunch. I would encourage everyone to take a bag lunch from home and invest half an hour in reading, writing, walking, and so forth. There alone you will have found about one hundred fifteen additional hours per year. What could be done in those one hundred fifteen hours? That capsule of time could result in a newly written book within approximately two years of such a half-hour daily snippet. Or you could have read forty new books. Or walked some two hundred thirty miles. Imagine that!

We waste so much time in front of the television each night. Let's assume a person watches four hours of TV per night. In those four hours he is bombarded with about one-and-a-half hours of commercials— wasteful, time-eliminating commercials that rob you of over five hundred hours per year! *Five hundred* great hours that could instead be invested in learning a new field, taking up a new hobby, writing two new books, doing a thousand Sudoku or crossword puzzles. Or you could have read at least a hundred and fifty new books!

You get the idea. We so readily allow time to control us instead of controlling it. I am not saying that time management is easy. There are many unique variables in each person's life that make it a challenge. But if you can carve out time each day—and I'm sure if you try hard enough, you can—you will discover the world of difference it can make.

Let's assume we had a contest in which anyone who could systematically carve out forty minutes per day, document it, and use it in a productive way for one year would win $50,000. I guarantee that 50 percent of the contest participants would qualify for the $50,000 reward. You see, it just takes the right amount of motivation. Could you qualify? I bet you could.

We are each capable of greatness. Remember, we were born to achieve greatness. It's just that somewhere along the way, we were convinced, little by little, that we were not capable of greatness. Somewhere along the way, we settled, maybe for the sake of comfort, or because we got tired, or we were just satisfied that we had enough. But we settled for less than greatness.

A man must know his destiny. If he does not recognize it, then he is lost. By this I mean, once twice, or at the very most, three times, fate will reach out and tap a man on the shoulder. If he has the imagination, he will turn around. And fate will point out to him what fork in the road he should take, [and] if he has the guts, he will take it.

—General George S. Patton (1885-1945)
American general during World War II

The most effective tool I have used in almost thirty-five years in business is the "Things to Do List." Time management means maximizing your efforts before the whistle blows marking the end of your workday. At closing time, are you satisfied that your important tasks for the day were accomplished?

I can remember getting sidetracked on some workdays. On those days, I had failed, for whatever reason, to use the "Things to Do List." During those workdays and after the day was over, I felt like a ship lost at sea, with no real direction. A ship or an airplane must have a map to follow, a destination, a time frame for travel, and an anticipated time of arrival. A "Things to Do List" provides just such a guideline, no matter what business you are in, as you write down items that it's important to finish that day, placing them in numbered order of importance.

The most pleasurable part of my day is when I finish a task and cross it off my list. I call that crossing-off a "Happy Celebration." The mind needs positive reinforcement, and "Happy Celebrations," to me, are positive reinforcements that I am worthwhile, I have achieved a small goal, and I am slowly getting to my ultimate task-achieving destination—the finish line for that day. Make sure the items on the list are listed in importance order, and there should be an achievable amount of items listed.

Many years ago, while running Bethlehem Steel, Charles Schwab called in a production consultant. The consultant, Ivy Lee, said, "In five minutes I can show you an idea to maximize your productivity." He proceeded to show Schwab the "Things to Do List" concept. He told Schwab to use it and have his workers use it for several weeks. If Schwab found he liked the idea, only then should he send Lee a check for whatever he thought the idea was worth. After several weeks, Schwab sent the consultant a check for $25,000, along with a letter telling Ivy Lee that his list idea was the most profitable thing, from a money standpoint, that he had ever learned.

The opposite of crossing off a task from my list and having a "Happy Celebration" in my mind, creating positive reinforcement and a sense of self-worth, is frustration and disorganized, haphazard thinking. The mind, after not achieving the tasks needed for the day due to lack of direction, becomes convinced it has failed—yes, failed—to do what was necessary. That negative reaction gets stored in the mind of the person with no plan of attack. Can you imagine a general leading troops in a war with no real plan of action? That would be "suicidal thinking."

This technique and many other ideas make up the spokes of the "success wheel" that will take you past all the average people who are convinced that they don't need any help, that they are fine operating according to the status quo, without any further growth.

I, on the other hand, am learning every day. Just recently I was able to learn valuable investment advice from someone less than half my age. I listened with an open mind to something I had previously taken for granted as being a poor investment. But with my ears wide open and my eyes focused on opportunity, I learned that the particular investment was indeed very valuable for a certain type of investor.

Anyone who stops learning is old, whether this happens at twenty or eighty. Anyone who keeps on learning not only remains young, but becomes constantly more valuable regardless of physical capacity.

—**Harvey Ullman,** author

An Intense, Burning Desire Propels Evil People, Too

Evil people, dictators, mass murderers, and some master thieves have used the same principles that the truly successful employ. They, too, are driven toward a goal. Some are extremely successful at achieving great fortunes, or mass killings and destruction, which in their world is considered tremendous success.

One such individual was Pablo Emilio Escobar. Escobar was a Colombian drug lord and leader of one of the most powerful criminal organizations ever built. He was born in 1949, and by the 1980s, he controlled a vast empire of drugs. He made billions of dollars, was once listed as the seventh richest man in the world, and was said to have been responsible for thousands of murders. At the age of forty-four, in 1993, he was shot dead by police.

Was it a great mind gone wrong? If channeled correctly, motivated properly, and maybe shown more love, could he have been a brilliant success for the good of humanity?

Many other people have performed fantastically evil deeds. There must be some extraordinary talent deep within the recesses of a mind filled with evil—a talent that could have done much good but, for some reason, bent toward evil.

Some killers or master thieves are so consumed with their own goals of greed or murder or fraud that they are motivated to work until they have "succeeded." One such intensely driven man was Bernard L. Madoff, an affable and charismatic investment genius who, over a period of more than twenty years, swindled thousands of investors out of more than $50 billion. He was so smooth at what he did, so brilliant in deceit, that no one ever knew he was stealing mega billions. He was evil in the worst possible meaning of the word, but he was motivated—he was driven. Destroying the financial lives of thousands, many of whom were senior citizens, didn't faze him. In the end, he merely smiled, not caring about what he had done.

I could only wonder: What if he had just applied his talents in a more useful way?

The evil that men do lives after them; the good is oft interred with their bones.

—**William Shakespeare** (1564-1616), English poet and playwright

---

We Are Each Born into This World Destined for Greatness!

Mariano Rivera is the greatest relief pitcher who ever put on a Major League Baseball uniform. Mariano was born on November 11, 1969, in Panama City. He grew up poor in a place where baseball gloves were made out of pieces of cardboard and a bat was made from the straightest limb of a tree.

He started out working, like his father, as a fisherman—grueling work with impossibly long hours. But hard work and dedication didn't faze Mariano. And when playing baseball, his dedication and work ethic ran deep.

Mariano couldn't speak English, but baseball is a universal game that knows no language, and Mariano was judged by what he did on the field.

Perhaps it was his poor upbringing, or his strong work ethic. Maybe it was the lure of coming to America, where great success was possible for a poor boy from a very poor country. Whatever it was, Mariano worked harder and longer than most other players. For more than fifteen years, Mariano has built up a baseball record as a relief pitcher that no one will probably ever match: over 525 saves and over a thousand strike-outs. He has pitched over one thousand innings and appeared in over nine hundred seventeen Major League games. And that is his record in only regular-season games. Mariano has, at age forty, been on five World Series Championship teams. Surely, he will be inducted into the Baseball Hall of Fame one day.

Chapter Twenty-Five

Stress Can Kill;
Learn How to Defuse It

The last great freedom we have is the freedom to choose our attitude under any given set of circumstances.

—Viktor Frankl (1905-1997) ,
Austrian neurologist and psychiatrist; Holocaust survivor

It has been proven that too much stress, if left unchecked, can kill or result in various health problems, some very severe.

We live in times of hectic days and nights, where the world revolves extremely fast all around us. News travels across the globe in mere seconds. Everything is instant—instant-messaging through texting over cell phones and the Internet, instant funds transfer into and out of our bank accounts. It's as if we are all racing toward something, but we don't even know what it is. The result is too much stress.

We are also stressed out over threats that bombard us every day— the doom and gloom that everyone keeps reminding us about. People walk around in fear instead of enjoying their lives. There is the threat of wars overseas, fear that some of our troops will be killed at the hands of terrorists.

Stress and worry can be likened to a deep-seated splinter in our finger or foot. The painful splinter eventually results in throbbing pain.

The pain grabs our attention, signaling to our brain that something must be done.

Stress and worry attacks the brain ruthlessly. The brain flashes thoughts of distress to our conscious mind. The flashing impulses destroy all good thoughts we are trying to experience during the day. But what is the alternative? We can't get rid of all the stressors. So how can we keep the personal effects of stress under control?

Worry Analyzed

Let's break down what most worry consists of:

- 40 percent of all things that we worry about never come to pass;
- 30 percent of all our worries involve past decisions that cannot be changed;
- 12 percent of worries focus on criticism from others who spoke because they felt inferior;
- 10 percent is related to our health, which gets worse when we worry;
- Only 8 percent of all worries could be described as "legitimate" causes for concern.

So, it can be established that 92 percent of our worry is useless and self-destructive.

Stress and worry have been linked to memory loss in some senior citizens. There are medical reasons why the brain does not handle worry and long-term stress very well: Stress can cause many health issues, and once the stress is eliminated or controlled, the symptoms are often eliminated, though long-term worry and stress can have permanent effects on memory loss.

I believe that one day many Alzheimer's cases will be linked to some traumatic, stressful periods in the patient's life. This is my own opinion and has no medical-research data to back it up. But I believe that when spouses lose their lifelong partner, the way they deal with that traumatic time determines their own health issues. If they are wholly devastated by the loss and grieve deeply over a long period of time, they tend to bring on many health problems—often including dementia.

Medical research has proven that psychological stress can result in bodily pain and many types of health issues. There is something inbred in all humans that has been referred to as the "fight or flight mechanism." For many thousands of years, when we sense a threat, the body reacts in fight or flight mode, either one of which activates the nervous system and prompts the adrenal glands to push out adrenaline, cortisol, and other hormones that prepare the body for the fight or flight needed for survival.

The results, other than additional strength, are tensing up of the muscles, slowing down of the digestive tract, constricting of the blood vessels, and racing of the heart. If we were being chased by lions and tigers, all this adrenaline would come in handy, but we do not need this concoction of chemicals pumping through our bodies on a continual basis today.

Stress, worry, and rushing to and fro can pump harmful chemical mixes through our bodies. So how do we deal with all this useless worry, stress, rushing around, and panic?

Don't wait until everything is just right. It will never be perfect. There will always be challenges, obstacles and less-than-perfect conditions. So what. Get started now. With each step you take, you will grow stronger and stronger, more and more skilled, more and more self-confident, and more and more successful.

—Mark Victor Hansen (b. 1948),
American motivational speaker and author

How to Beat Stress

Attitude is crucial. To shift your attitude in such a way as to minimize the effects of stress, try the following:

- Realize that 92 percent of all worry is useless and self-destructive.
- Exercise to calm the mind and body; physical exercise releases certain brain chemicals that naturally relax the body, while mental exercise helps us to focus on more positive things.
- Repeat self-esteem affirmations such as:
- "And this, too, shall pass."
- "I will be successful; it is inevitable."
- "I am better than this thing."
- "Action beats worry every day."
- Put it all in perspective; work it out in your mind. Is it really that important?
- Put your mind into a happier time of your life, sometime in the past, and think of why you felt happier then.
- Put your faith in a Higher Being:
- "The Lord is my Shepherd. I shall not fear."
- Count your blessings, visualize all you have going for you—start with your eyes, ears, mind, arms, legs, etc.

Can the Mind Turn from Negative to Positive Quickly?

Is it possible to turn someone's attitude from negative to positive at a moment's notice? A person with the weight of the world on their shoulders can become happy and positive immediately. Let's take the example of someone who went to the accountant to do his yearly taxes. He expected to have to pay a couple thousand dollars to the IRS. He had been worrying about the tax problem for months. But because of the economy and decreased income for the year, the accountant told him he could instead expect to receive a refund of $6,000.

What just happened? One negative thought-impulse has just been replaced, rather suddenly, with a very positive thought impulse. This new positive impulse will keep sending positive thought impulses to the conscious from the subconscious for quite some time.

You see, positives can replace negatives rapidly. And negatives can replace positives just as fast. You have to work at it every day, so count your blessings daily.

Today is a gift—that is why it is called The Present.

—Often attributed to **Eleanor Roosevelt** (1884-1962),
former First Lady of the United States

This little story, passed around a bit on the Internet, just may change your thinking:

Two men, both seriously ill, occupied the same hospital room. One man was allowed to sit up in his bed for an hour each afternoon to help drain the fluid from his lungs. His bed was next to the room's only window. The other man had to spend all his time flat on his back.

The men talked for hours on end. They spoke of their wives and families, their homes, their jobs, their involvement in the military service, where they had visited while on vacation…And every afternoon, when the man in the bed by the window could sit up, he would pass the time by describing to his roommate all the things he could see outside the window. The man in the other bed began to live for those one-hour periods where his world would be broadened and enlivened by all the activity and color of the world outside.

The window overlooked a park with a lovely lake. Ducks and swans played on the water while children sailed their model boats. Young lovers walked arm in arm amid flowers of every color, and a fine view of the city skyline could be seen in the distance. As the man by the window described all this in exquisite detail, the man on the other side of the room would close his eyes and imagine the picturesque scene.

One warm afternoon, the man by the window described a parade passing by. Although the other man could not hear the band, he could see it in his mind's eye as the gentleman by the window portrayed it with descriptive words.

Days, weeks, and months passed.

One morning, the day nurse arrived to bring water for their baths only to find the lifeless body of the man by the window, who had died peacefully in his sleep. She was saddened and called the hospital attendants to take the body away.

As soon as it seemed appropriate, the other man asked if he could be moved next to the window. The nurse was happy to make the switch, and after making sure he was comfortable, she left him alone.

Slowly, painfully, he propped himself up on one elbow to take his first look at the real world outside. He strained to slowly turn to look out the window beside the bed.

It faced a blank wall.

The man asked the nurse what could have compelled his deceased roommate to describe such wonderful things outside this window. The nurse responded that the man was blind and could not even see the wall. She said, "Perhaps he just wanted to encourage you."

The moral of the story? There is tremendous happiness in making others happy, despite our own situations.

Don't Stress Out over Failures

Don't ever stress out over past failures or over the possibility of future failures; we have been failing since the beginning of time. Imagine the first time someone tried to create fire. How many times did he get burned before a flame actually shot forth? How about the first person who tried to eat a cactus plant? You know, it has all been tried before.

People tried honey made from bees, and perhaps ate the bee also. No doubt someone somewhere has tried to eat bark, dirt, and rocks. Someone tried to climb a tree and fly from it like a bird. Of course, they all failed. When we were babies, we tried to walk and fell, maybe even hurting ourselves. We tried to ride a bike and roller-skate, only to fall and scrape our knees. You see, nothing that was ever accomplished became a success immediately without some sort of failure.

Since the beginning of time, each new generation has improved on prior generations' great failures, as well as on prior generations' great new successes. Improvements, reinventions—better, stronger, faster. In fact, we are each reinventing ourselves on a daily basis. We are evolving, getting better, smarter, stronger. We must continue to grow.

Immigrants are a great example of each new generation reinventing itself. Imagine coming to America as a foreigner, maybe not knowing the language well or not at all. Not every immigrant succeeds. Many fail. But each new immigrant reinvents, improves, does it better than those who preceded him or her.

It is said that legal immigrants who come to the United States are four times more likely to become millionaires than those born here. Expectation to succeed is huge. The brain expects and works toward only the successful outcome it is convinced of.

We should realize that failure is just a big part of life and is the predecessor to all success. We should not be thrown by failure that presents itself to us as we travel our long road to achievement. Look at the first time someone gets behind the wheel of a car to learn how to drive, or the first time someone takes a flying lesson. I remember trying to fly a plane while using a flight simulator on my computer. I must have crashed that plane twenty times in a row, but slowly I learned to land the plane properly. Can you imagine if we could succeed at everything the very first time we attempted to do something?

The man who has done his level best, and who is conscious that he has done his best, is a success, even though the world may write him down as a failure.

—**B.C. Forbes** (1880-1954), Scottish financial journalist, founder of *Forbes Magazine*

I am personally driven to accomplish as much as I can in the unknown allotment of time in my hourglass. We have been blessed with life. We all begin the glorious journey of life from the same starting gate. Some will start fast and furiously; some will start life slowly but increase their efforts along the way; others will burn out like a short, thin candle.

Nature Shows Us a Good Example

Each fall, Monarch butterflies begin an incredible migration, journeying across North America to a hilltop in Mexico. They focus on their destination, not on all the difficulties along the way. Each day, the butterflies take their bearings and set off, allowing instinct and desire to steer them toward their goal. They accept whatever comes; some winds blow them off course, while others speed them along their way. The butterflies keep flying until, one day, they finally arrive.

When it's all over, all said and done, what impact will my life have had on this world?

—JPC

How Do You See the World?

Three hundred years ago, Christopher Wren, who designed St. Paul's Cathedral in London, wrote about three men he had spoken to as they were helping to build his creation. He asked the first worker what his job was, to which the worker wearily replied, "I'm laying bricks. Can't you see that?" Wren moved along and asked a second worker the same question. "I'm just earning a living," the second worker snapped back. The architect then asked the same question of a third worker, who was whistling away while he worked, and he got a very different response: "I'm building a cathedral!" he said proudly.

Attitude is what we eat, breathe, and live. Why shouldn't it be cultivated into something positive? It will show in your eyes. It will be reflected in the way you walk and smile. We can choose to be different, choose to be positive, and set an example.

Nothing can stop the man with the right mental attitude from achieving his goal; nothing on earth can help the man with the wrong mental attitude.

—**Thomas Jefferson** (1743-1826), 3rd President of the United States

Thomas Kinkade is an artist who has sold more canvases than any other painter in history. He is known to many as the "Painter of Light." Kinkade's empire is worth more than $100 million. He employs hundreds of workers, and there are more than three hundred Kinkade galleries selling his paintings each day.

Thomas Kinkade was born in 1958 and grew up in the small town of Placerville, California. At the age of five, his parents divorced, but Kinkade knew he had a special talent. He has stated, "I was always the kid that could draw. I had this talent, and it was the one thing that gave me some kind of dignity in the midst of my personal environment, because growing up, I was very impoverished."

At the age of sixteen, Kinkade was apprenticed under a well-known artist, Glen Wessels. Kinkade went on at an early age to become a painter of unique style who has distanced himself from all other painters. He found a niche, a way of making it appear that electric lights are shining from within each painting.

Down deep, every soul has a hidden longing, impulse, and ambition to do something fine and enduring ... if you are willing, great things are possible to you.

—**Grenville Kleiser** (1868-1935), Inspirational author

We Are Each Born into This World Destined for Greatness!

Jim Henson, creator of the world-famous "Muppets," was born on September 24, 1936, in Mississippi. In the early 1950s, he got very involved with puppetry and soon came up with the Muppets. With its debut in 1969 starring many of Henson's special puppets, the kids' television show *Sesame Street* made the Muppets—and Henson—a household name.

Henson's Muppets are as popular today as they were in the early days. And even though Henson passed on in 1990, his son continued to grow the Muppet enterprise.

In 2004, the Disney Corporation purchased Jim Henson's Muppets company for almost $700 million. A hand, a puppet, an imagination, a dream, a desire, and plenty of hard work led to a unique idea that has lasted already for more than fifty years, and the Muppets family is still going strong.

Chapter Twenty-Six

And This, Too, Shall Pass

Don't waste your life in doubts and fears; spend yourself on the work before you, well assured that the right performance of this hour's duties will be the best preparation for the hours or ages that follow it.

—Ralph Waldo Emerson (1803-1882),
American philosopher, essayist, poet

We are each guilty of worrying at some time in our life. Some people worry constantly. Worry can cause people to overeat or under-eat, or it can cause the body to revolt against itself. Worry can cause excessive acid to churn up in a person's stomach, which can lead to serious conditions. Some worry so much that they always have to be close to a restroom.

Why do we worry? Why does that "worry splinter" settle inside our subconscious mind, causing constant vibrations of problems we suspect will be critical? We already know that 92 percent of all worry is useless and self-defeating, and that most things worried about will never come to pass.

And This, Too, Shall Pass!

All things, good and bad, will ultimately pass. Every time I have found myself worrying about my latest health issue, be it excruciating back pain that lasted weeks or a knee that gave me serious concerns for over a month, something has shocked me back to reality.

Don't sweat the small stuff, and it's all small stuff.

—**Richard Carlson** (1961-2006),
American author and motivational speaker

The majority of what you presently consider problems, one year from today, will seem minuscule, unimportant. When compared to serious problems that exist in the world, most of our problems are, in reality, insignificant. Of course, we believe our problems are very important. Like my tremendous backache, or my knee that throbbed for weeks for which I thought I would need an operation, most so-called "important" problems slowly disappear. The strange thing is this: When you look around yourself, really study the people you encounter on a daily basis, you will see many people far worse off than you. This always wakes me right up, and the problems I thought were so severe just slowly evaporate.

There are many people who sit late at night when they are alone and fester with worry. Perhaps they eat too much or bite their nails endlessly while worrying about a host of things—the same things they always seem to worry about. It is a known fact that when a person over-worries, the body reacts as if threatened. The brain, when overwhelmed with worry, releases a stress hormone called cortisol, which can cause excess belly fat and possibly heart disease. Over time, excessive worry can have a huge effect on memory loss. The human brain is like a manufacturing plant, producing a whole concoction of chemicals. In short, they can cure you or ultimately kill you. Therefore, it is paramount that what you feed your mind be positive and not negative, destructive thoughts.

Once again we come back to positive affirmations. One powerful thing that can separate you from the mass of people who walk this earth in a fog of worry is your positive thinking, which will keep you inoculated against the disease of negative influences and negative thoughts.

Self-Talk Affirmations

I suggest the following as brief positive affirmations:

- *"Stop! Stop worrying. Ninety-two percent of all worry is useless and self-defeating and draining. Stop! Stop worrying!"*
- *"I am good, I am secure, I can overcome anything!"*
- *"If the worst happens, will I still have my mind? Will I still have my eyes, my ears, my legs? Will I still have the people who love me? Then I truly have it all."*
- *"The Lord is my Shepherd; I will not fear! Let me take this problem and give it over to the Lord."*
- *"I feel healthy, I feel blessed, I really do have it made."*
- *"And this, too, shall pass!"*

Worry a little bit every day and in a lifetime you will lose a couple of years. If something is wrong, fix it if you can. But train yourself not to worry. Worry never fixes anything.

—Mary Hemingway (1908-1986), American journalist

Remember, positive affirmations will raise the impenetrable shield that protects your subconscious mind from being infected by all the negativity in the world. You will remember, that we each, on average, have sixty thousand thoughts per day. And most of those thoughts and the talk all around us is negative in nature. Therefore, your shield must be raised high and strong to protect you. But like the bodybuilder, we must exercise that positive self-talk every morning, noon, and night. It will change your life, but only if you will yourself to accept the change.

Desire is the starting point of all achievement, not a hope, not a wish, but a keen pulsating desire which transcends everything.

—Napoleon Hill (1883-1970), American author

Research has shown that almost 90 percent of all doctor visits are for conditions caused by or compounded by stress. This includes such conditions as high blood pressure, diabetes, autoimmune deficiencies, back pain, stomach disorders, and much more.

It is important to remember that nobody is perfect, nothing in life is perfect, and we surely do not have to be perfect. All we have to be is the best that we can be for ourselves.

I believe the outstanding successes of our world have simply planned to be successful. They consciously or subconsciously planned, systematically, to succeed. If you want to be different, then you must begin to act and think differently. Not just today, not just while you are reading an inspiring book, but every day for the rest of your life.

But here is an intriguing fact: 80 percent of all your neighbors will not will themselves to change; 80 percent will not work at something new and systematic for the rest of their lives, even if it means that changing could lead them to greatness. Be different. Make a conscious effort everyday to be different than everyone else. Stand up, Stand out, Be different, and you will succeed with this new attitude.

Fear is conquered by action. When we challenge our fears, we defeat them. When we fight against our difficulties, they lose their hold on us. When we dare to face the things that scare us, we open the door to freedom.

—Author unknown

Helping Yourself to Be Your Best

It is not the critic that counts; not the man who points out how the strong man stumbles or where the doer of deeds could have done better. The credit belongs to the man who is actually in the arena, whose face is marred by dust and sweat and blood; who strives valiantly; who errs, and comes short again and again, because there is no effort without error and shortcoming; who knows the great enthusiasms, the great devotions; who spends himself in a worthy cause; who at best knows in the end the triumph of high achievement. And at worst, if he fails, at least fails while daring greatly, so that his place shall never be with those cold and timid souls who know neither victory nor defeat.

—Theodore Roosevelt (1858-1919),
26th President of the United States

I have just found out something most of us have suspected for years. It has been proven that sleep deprivation can have very adverse effects on our bodies. Just cutting sleep time from seven hours nightly to six hours will increase the likelihood of a heart attack. In fact, for those overactive-lifestyle people, here is a scary statistic: Sleeping for less than five hours leads to a 38 percent increase in heart disease. Sleeping for less than six hours leads to an 18 percent increase in heart disease. The person who sleeps only five to six hours nightly has an increased risk of high blood pressure by 350 to 500 percent. The ideal sleep duration per night is from seven to eight hours.

A habit, we explained earlier, is formed in approximately twenty days. You can form a new habit within twenty days from today. Not many people like to exercise. I want to stress, once again, the importance of exercising, specifically by walking. The benefits are too great to ignore. Walking works and tones up many muscle groups, including calf muscles, ankles, hamstrings, hip flexors, buttocks, abdominal muscles, arm and shoulder muscles, and more. It has been said that walking exercises every part of the body.

Walking, for me, is a great time to think, come up with ideas, and work out solutions to problems I am trying to solve. Walking will extend your life; it actually cuts the risk of heart disease substantially. Walking will also benefit you as it:

- improves circulation,
- helps breathing,
- combats depression,
- bolsters the immune system,
- helps prevent osteoporosis,

- helps prevent diabetes,
- helps control weight.

In fact, twenty minutes of walking per day will result in the average person burning 32,120 calories each year. Not bad! Imagine burning all those calories and toning up, too.

The chemicals that the brain releases when one exercises are endorphins. These chemicals are a natural pain reducer and give one a euphoric feeling. There is no doubt that the daily habit of walking will change your life for the better. You will enjoy a sounder, more relaxed state of sleep. You will have fewer pains and a sharper mind, and you'll feel better about yourself and the world around you.

I do my best walking in a large local mall. It is temperature-controlled for year-round walking enjoyment. The mall also offers so many visual benefits, including young, smiling children, a pet store with all breeds of puppies, and older people who remind me each day not to delay on my goals, as time waits for no man.

We were each blessed with a fabulous, unique miracle of a body; why not cherish and pamper that body? Why not maximize its working capacity and longevity?

I would rather be ashes than dust! I would rather that my spark should burn out in a brilliant blaze than it should be stifled by dry rot. I would rather be a superb meteor, every atom of me in magnificent glow, than a sleepy and permanent planet. The proper function of man is to live, not to exist. I shall not waste my days in trying to prolong them. I shall use my time.

—**Jack London** (1876-1916), American author

Breathe a Sigh of Relief

Breathing is a real art. I don't mean breathing air simply to live; I mean relearning breathing to reduce stress and to reinforce our subconscious mind. Experts say that most of us do not breathe properly. Sounds strange since we all breathe quite naturally just to survive. But it is true.

It has been said that many ailments can be cured by relearning the proper technique of breathing. I learned this years ago, quite by accident, when I found a computer site that used a colorful ball that contracted and expanded showing me at what pace and how deeply I should be breathing. The goal was that by breathing more deeply while observing the expanding ball, one could deeply relax the mind and body more, and even lower blood pressure readings.

It is said that to breathe properly we must breathe like a baby. In other words, we all knew how to breathe properly at birth, but somewhere along the way, we got sidetracked. To breathe properly for optimum stress-releasing benefits, first place a hand on your stomach. Now breathe slowly and deeply through your nose. Now exhale deeply through your mouth. If you feel your stomach rise and fall, you are breathing correctly. So breathe like a baby, and like a baby, you will have few problems.

I like to take the deep-breathing exercise a bit further. What I do is add positive self-help affirmations to the breathing routine. Here is the exercise:

- First, go to a quiet place and sit in a relaxing chair.
- Now breathe in deeply through your nose.
- Now hold it for five seconds.
- Next, while you exhale slowly through your mouth for at least five seconds, say a statement such as
  - "I release all the stress from my body!"
- As you once again breathe in through your nose, say a statement such as
  - "I draw in all the positive, the good of the world!"
- Breathe out slowly, through your mouth, with a statement such as
  - "The Lord is my Shepherd; I shall not fear!"

- Breathe in, through your nose, and say
  - "I feel great, I feel wonderful, I have the world by the tail."

Do this exercise each night for ten minutes. It will change your life.

Without change, something sleeps inside us and seldom awakens. The sleeper must awaken.

—**Frank Herbert** (1920-1986), American science fiction author

You can choose whatever statements you wish when you do your breathing exercises, as well as in your self-help affirmations throughout the day. But another statement I have used to reduce stress while breathing deeply is this one:

Breathing in: "I draw energy and strength, and nothing will stand in my way!"

Breathing out: "I now release this problem from my mind, as 92 percent of all worry is useless!"

We Are Each Born into This World Destined for Greatness!

Milton S. Hershey was born in 1857 in Derry Church, Pennsylvania. Like many people of that time, Hershey had little formal education. He was a driven man, but like many, he had to overcome obstacles. At age nineteen, Hershey attempted to start his own candy business, but after six years, he failed. He went to work for a caramel maker, learned the business, and tried to open his own caramel store, but it, too, failed. By age thirty, he was nearly bankrupt. He began working as an apprentice for a candy maker.

But Hershey was no quitter. He opened another caramel business in Pennsylvania and, this time, became a success. His business soon employed 1,400 people. In 1900, he sold the caramel-making business for an astounding figure, especially for his day, of $1 million. Hershey was now on a new mission.

He had been intrigued with the art of making chocolate after attending the World's Fair Columbian Exposition in Chicago. So he purchased some machines from Germany and began experimenting with different recipes. After a while, Hershey perfected his recipe for milk chocolate. In 1903, he began producing milk chocolate under the Hershey name. The rest is history. Hershey built an empire in the chocolate business. He went on to build a community where his workers would be housed. He built an amusement park, started an elementary school, and even transferred much of his wealth to be used to benefit local schools.

The town of Hershey, Pennsylvania, to this day is a huge attraction. Milton Hershey is a great example of how someone with little formal education can go on to be one of the most successful and motivating entrepreneurs the world has ever known.

Every great dream begins with a dreamer. Always remember, you have within you the strength, the patience, and the passion to reach for the stars to change the world.

—Harriet Tubman (ca. 1820-1913)
African-American abolitionist, humanitarian and Union spy

Chapter Twenty-Seven

Stand Out from the Crowd with Creative Visualization

A man can be as great as he wants to be. If you believe in yourself and have the courage, the determination, the dedication, the competitive drive, and if you are willing to sacrifice the little things in life and pay the price for the things that are worthwhile, it can be done.

—**Vince Lombardi** (1913-1970), American football coach

In this world of hustle and bustle, the average person's life is very hectic. It's almost like we are all riding a carousel that is spinning out of control at one hundred miles per hour and we can't jump off. It's a wonder many people find the time to achieve goals or to improve themselves.

We now live in the world of MySpace, Twitter, and Facebook. Although these online social-networking sites are great for communicating with friends and relatives, they can also become habit-forming, addictive wastes of huge blocks of time. I fear that many people will achieve less than they otherwise would have in exchange for the attention and reinforcement that come through communicating too much on sites such as these. Where will it end?

On the other hand, I could be wrong! Even the great Michelangelo said, "I am still learning."

If confined to a very small allotment of time on a daily basis, it could be

psychologically beneficial. There will no doubt be a study someday showing that the improvement to self-esteem, the attention gained from others, and the social interaction offered by such sites can be useful, if not abused.

So, in the fast-moving world we live in, the only real relaxation and total quiet time to ourselves is when we close our eyes each night. As we fall off to sleep, honking horns, rushing trains and buses, and all other noises fade away. It is truly "our quiet time."

Since we spend almost one-third of our lives sleeping, recharging our bodies so we can be our best for those sixteen or so hours we are awake, needing to be functional and alert, how can we maximize this precious time? Is it possible to use the window of time while we fall off to sleep more efficiently? Yes! We can maximize this time before deep sleep with a form of relaxation called "Creative Visualization."

Total relaxation methods of various kinds have been practiced in many countries for centuries. Methods such as meditation, hypnosis, biofeedback, and others have been used to help the brain deal with various forms of illness. Relaxation helps the body heal from within, but it has innumerable other benefits. A study was done at Harvard University and the Prevention Medicine Research Institute of San Francisco. It showed that patients who practiced relaxation techniques on a regular basis had better control of their illnesses and were able to decrease their medications.

Creative Visualization is the practice of attempting to alter your thoughts in order to positively affect the world around you. Through this relaxation technique, we quiet down the world and open up the subconscious mind for deeper programming.

Benefits of the Creative Visualization Method of Relaxation

Benefits of this technique include:

- Muscle fatigue and tension reduced;
- Increased circulation of oxygen to the muscles;
- Leads to a deeper level of physical relaxation;
- Reduction of "fight or flight" response;
- Reduction of pain, insomnia, headaches, and fatigue;
- Better mental focus;
- Easier to create new, good habits and to break bad ones;
- Less stress and anxiety;
- Better reinforcement of mental self-worth;
- Ability to connect more directly with the all-powerful subconscious mind and program it more deeply for later use.

Any thought that is passed on to the subconscious often enough and convincingly enough is finally accepted.

—Robert Collier (1885-1950), American author

Over the years, placebos (fake treatment) given in place of real medication have at times cured people of various ailments. In one study of topical treatments for baldness, hair actually grew on a fair number of placebo patients in the study group, because those individuals' belief was that intense. In other studies, the placebo seemed to give people many of the side effects that the actual medications gave the patients who took them. And in recent studies with regard to pain medication, patients who took the fake pills claimed to feel as good as or better than those who took actual pain medication. Using brain scans on the placebo patients, it was determined that because the patient believed so strongly in the placebo's effectiveness, their own brains produced pain relief. The scans showed clearly that the patients' brains produced endorphins, the body's natural painkiller. Because of belief and expectation, the body willed itself to feel better. And the benefits were long-lasting. As long as the patient believed and the doctor kept giving the fake medication in a positive manner, the patient continued showing improvement for years.

Belief is the magic potion each of us possesses. Practiced daily, it will separate you from those poor souls who only believe after seeing.

—JPC

If you truly want to help yourself excel in life and business—if you believe that your powerful mind, if programmed properly, can change your life—then there exists no more powerful tool than a form of self-relaxation called creative visualization.

This exercise, if you believe strongly enough, will change your life. But like all other exercises and affirmations, it must be maintained. It must become a part of your life. In return, your health, happiness, family, and business life will benefit tremendously.

Instructions for Using the Creative Visualization Method of Relaxation

1. Choose a very quiet room, preferably your bedroom at sleep time. Lie down or sit comfortably.
2. Close your eyes. Eliminate all worry and outside thoughts and concerns of work, school, family.
3. Next, breathe in deeply through your nose while counting five full seconds. Now breathe out through your nose for five full seconds. Feel your lungs empty. Repeat this sequence for five sets.
4 Next, do a body scan. With your eyes still closed, visualize your body parts going limp one by one. Start with your toes; feel them go limp. Next, feel your legs; think deeply and feel them totally relaxed, almost asleep. Don't move on to the next body part until you feel the heavy weight of each body part. Continue the breathing method.

5. Next, visualize your back, then your fingers, arms, shoulders, neck, mouth, eyes, all slowly going limp and totally relaxed. Feel your scalp; visualize it totally relaxed. Your body now feels heavier and more relaxed than ever before.

6. Visualize the following series of colors one at a time, not moving on to the next until you visualize each one: yellow, green, blue, purple, and red. If you need to, visualize the colors in clothes, M&Ms, shoes, stop signs, etc.—anything that helps you see the color. Keep breathing with the same method.

7. Visualize being at the top of a concrete staircase that is very high, overlooking a beach and ocean, with beautiful blue skies and white puffs of clouds.

8. Slowly descend the staircase one step at a time. Notice the bluest sky, whitest clouds, the sand and waves.

9. You are now at the base of the staircase, standing on the sand. Feel the warmth of the sand, the heat of the sun on your body. Now you can hear the ocean waves. Visualize the waves slowly coming to the shore.

10. You are totally relaxed. You are now very receptive to any suggestions into your subconscious mind. You feel almost euphoric. Stay awake and think of the following statements one by one:
    - "I feel healthy, I feel happy, I feel terrific!"
    - "I will be successful; it's inevitable because my aggressiveness will lead to opportunities for my success!"
    - "Every day and in every way I am getting better and better!"
    - "Nothing at all can stop me if I truly believe!"

You will now fall off to a sound sleep, and you will rise in the morning refreshed and invigorated with tremendous energy to tackle whatever the world throws at you. Because now you have built up the mental shields that will defend against all the negativity that we are normally bombarded with on a daily basis, nothing negative can possibly penetrate this new optimism, belief, and inspiration.

We Are Each Born into This World Destined for Greatness!

Jim Carrey is a true "rags to riches" story. He grew up in Canada, living in a camper-van with his family. The family was poor, so Jim worked eight-hour shifts at a tire factory to contribute to the family income. He became a high school dropout and moved to Los Angeles to try and make it in comedy.

Jim worked as a regular at the Comedy Store in the 1980s and soon became Rodney Dangerfield's opening act. He later landed on the television show *In Living Color*.

Jim Carrey, the poor boy who once lived in a camper-van, now earns about $30 million per year in movie salaries. Was there a certain drive, a certain hunger for success? Don't ever think that Jim does not remember where he came from; perhaps that is the burning desire deep inside his heart.

I love success stories. But I especially love the rags-to-riches success stories that remind all of us that we, too, can become whatever we truly desire.

You, too, have now arrived at your new road to success, a road filled with motivation and inspiring thoughts that will lift you and carry you over the various hurdles you will inevitably encounter. And in the end, you will arrive at your finish line, your ultimate dream of success! Congratulations!

My Success Affirmations

Today I am born anew. Today is the most important day of my life because it represents the glorious and first day of my new life.

I now understand that I alone control my destiny, my success or my failure in this wondrous world of opportunity. Am I now capable, too, of greatness and fortune like those highly successful individuals I have learned about? For now I truly understand that I can accomplish anything I carefully program into my mind. Does not the immigrant cherish fully the American opportunity, knowing they must succeed and that failure is not an option in their newfound world? I will adopt a similar burning desire, and I will excel.

I am born anew. For now I realize that I am the greatest miracle in the world, unique to anyone ever born. No longer will I count the obstacles and drawbacks in my life. I now realize that, like the inventor who welcomes each new failure on the road to victory, so, too, shall I. For now I understand that each failure only brings me closer to the success I know will be mine.

Never again will I allow self-pity, doubt, or negativity to penetrate my new power-mind, protected by a new negativity-shield, for now I realize that 80 percent of all talk and actions around me will be negative. I now realize that negativity has been around since the caveman, and yet successful people always prevailed. I, too, shall prevail. I, too, will stand out from the crowd. I am a king and the world is my new kingdom, for now I realize that the knowledge I possess is worth more than all the riches of the world.

Today I possess an immense knowledge of how to change my life forever. It is a true celebration indeed because now I realize that the best is yet to be.

Just like the wind that graces the earth, never will I look back. Never will I revisit yesterday's problems and heartaches. They are dead. I will always look forward with a newfound, childlike excitement and energy.

Never again will I allow my life to be likened to a casino game of chance because I now understand that I alone take full responsibility for my results along the long road to success, and I vow to apply the principles I have learned along the way. It is a joy to travel the long road to success. I will savor every step, enjoying the rough as well as the easy road I encounter.

Today and everyday forward I will welcome each new day as a blessing from above, and I vow never again to squander such a precious gift, knowing that the richest king can never buy one more day of life. It is truly a gift from the Creator and shall never again be wasted.

Enthusiasm, I have learned, is contagious. And I know that if I project an enthusiastic, positive attitude to all whom I encounter each day, they, too, will be enthused and will spread it to others. And like all wealth shared with love, it no doubt will inspire me all the more.

I realize that I have choices in life:

I can feel happy, or I can feel sad.

I can act positive, or I can act in a negative manner.

I can succeed greatly, or I can settle for failure as an end result.

I can love all others I encounter, or carry around baggage of doom and gloom and aversion.

I choose to be different, to stand out and set an example that others will admire and want to emulate.

This is my new life. I am like a newborn, pure in heart and mind from prejudice, hatred, failure, or fear. And like a newborn, full of life and hope, I now understand that I, too, am unspoiled now in my mind. I now possess the great knowledge of the ages. For now I know that the mind controls the body, and the subconscious controls the conscious. As long as I feed the subconscious mind good, pure, and positive thoughts, the subconscious will radiate like the rays of the sun, thus renewing, invigorating, and warming me each day like the powerful rays of the sun. For this little-known secret of my subconscious is now part of my life, part of my daily routine. And with each new day that I take a breath of air, I, too, will begin it with positive self-suggestion statements.

My newfound positive-attitude shield will protect me from the arrows of negativity that kill off the spirit and drive off so many other people. I am different; I am new. I will apply the newfound knowledge I possess.

No longer will that negativity seep into my mind. I will not allow negativity to affect the computer-mind God gave me. I was born to be great. Greatness is my destiny.

From this day forward I will never again worry, for now I know that 92 percent of all worry is useless, self-defeating, and draining.

Like the seasons that change, I now understand that my emotions, too, change, and though I may not feel as happy one day, I know that in a day or two I could possibly be ecstatic. Like the cycles of the world, emotions change, and now my newfound knowledge is power I will be able to use.

With love in my eyes and heart, I will greet everyone I meet with sincere kindness. For now I understand that love alone will soften the coldest hearts of enemies and friends alike. And if I am to help others along the road to success, I must set an example of pure love and inspiration for all to follow. My new attitude will be my shield that will protect me from the dreaded arrows of negativity that kill off the spirit and drive off so many others. I am now different; I am new; I am driven.

And as someone who loves himself, I now vow to allow only good things to enter my mind and body, and to eliminate anything harmful from affecting me. I will ignore the surrounding negativity and indulgences that can harm this masterpiece-body that I have been born with. I now know that I am the greatest work of art in the world, a masterpiece that no money can ever duplicate.

I now vow that each new day will be carefully unwrapped and savored for the precious gift it represents. And in the end, I will know that I have made my Creator proud of what I have accomplished, and I will be able to look back, knowing that I have set a truly inspiring example and have made a lasting, positive difference in this great world of ours.

About the Author

John Paul Carinci has been a successful insurance executive and president of Carinci Insurance Agency, Inc., for 35 years.

John is also an author, songwriter, poet, and CEO of Better Off Dead Productions, Inc., a movie production company.

As a worldwide published author, some of John's other works include: *The Power of Being Different, In Exchange of Life, Share Your Mission #5, A Second Chance, The Psychic Boy Detective, Better Off Dead, Better Off Dead In Paradise,* and *A Gift from Above.* John is also co-writer of the screenplays: *Better Off Dead, A Second Chance,* and *Better Off Dead in Paradise,* which were all adapted from his novels, and may one day be produced as motion pictures.

John's first self-help book, *The Power of Being Different,* has been translated and published in many foreign countries.

Suggested Reading

The following are related books quoted from, or those which may bring additional light on strategies listed in this book.

You Can If You Think You Can!: by Norman Vincent Peale, Fireside, 1987.

Long Time No See: by Dr. No-Yong Park, Exposition Press

Success Through A Positive Mental Attitude: By Napoleon Hill and W. Clement Stone, Pocket Books, 1991.

The Greatest Salesman In The World: by Og Mandino, Bantam Books, 1983.

The Choice: by Og Mandino, Bantam Books, 1990.

The Power Of Your Subconscious Mind: by Dr. Joseph Murphy, Bantam Books, 2001.

The Magic Of Thinking Big: by David Schwartz, Fireside, 1987.

The Magic Of Believing: by Claude M. Bristol, Pocket Books, 1991.

David St. Clair's Lessons in Instant ESP: By David St. Clair, Signet, 1986.

Beyond Survival: by Gerald Coffee, Putnam Publishing Group, 1990.

The Conquest Of Happiness: by Bertrand Russell, Liveright Publishing, 1996.

The One Minute Manager: by Kenneth Blanchard & Spencer Johnson, Berkley Books, 1983.

In Search Of Excellence: by Tom Peters, Warner Books, 1988.

Heart Of A Champion: by Bob Richards, Books-on-Demand, 2004

21ˢᵗ Century Positioning: by Jack & Garry Kinder, Taylor Publishing, 1999

Don't Sweat The Small Stuff…and it's all small stuff: by Richard Carlson, Ph.D., Hyperion, 1997.

The Power Of Being Different: by John Paul Carinci, Author House, 2005

As A Man Thinketh: by James Allen, Tarcher, 2008

Chicken Soup For The Soul: by Jack Canfield, HCI, 2001

Think And Grow Rich: by Napoleon Hill, Fawcett Crest Books, 1960

Tuesdays With Morrie: by Mitch Albom, Broadway, 2002

The Last Lecture: by Randy Pausch, Ph,D, Hyperion, 2008

The Recreations Of A Country Parson: by A. Boyd, Alexander Strahan, 1867

O's Guide To Life: by Editors Of The Magazine, Oxmoor House, 2007

Putting The Power Of Your Subconscious Mind To Work: by Joseph Murphy, Prentice Hall Press, 2009

The Law Of Success: by Napoleon Hill, Ralston University Press, 1928

BUY A SHARE OF THE FUTURE IN YOUR COMMUNITY

These certificates make great holiday, graduation and birthday gifts that can be personalized with the recipient's name. The cost of one S.H.A.R.E. or one square foot is $54.17. The personalized certificate is suitable for framing and will state the number of shares purchased and the amount of each share, as well as the recipient's name. The home that you participate in "building" will last for many years and will continue to grow in value.

Here is a sample SHARE certificate:

THIS CERTIFIES THAT

YOUR NAME HERE

HAS INVESTED IN A HOME FOR A DESERVING FAMILY

1985-2010

TWENTY-FIVE YEARS OF BUILDING FUTURES
IN OUR COMMUNITY ONE HOME AT A TIME

1200 SQUARE FOOT HOUSE @ $65,000 = $54.17 PER SQUARE FOOT
This certificate represents a tax deductible donation. It has no cash value.

YES, I WOULD LIKE TO HELP!

I support the work that Habitat for Humanity does and I want to be part of the excitement! As a donor, I will receive periodic updates on your construction activities but, more importantly, I know my gift will help a family in our community realize the dream of homeownership. **I would like to SHARE in your efforts against substandard housing in my community!** *(Please print below)*

PLEASE SEND ME _____ SHARES at $54.17 EACH = $ $_____

In Honor Of: _____

Occasion: (Circle One) HOLIDAY   BIRTHDAY   ANNIVERSARY

OTHER: _____

Address of Recipient: _____

Gift From: _____ *Donor Address:* _____

Donor Email: _____

I AM ENCLOSING A CHECK FOR $ $_____ PAYABLE TO HABITAT FOR HUMANITY OR PLEASE CHARGE MY VISA OR MASTERCARD *(CIRCLE ONE)*

Card Number _____ Expiration Date: _____

Name as it appears on Credit Card _____ Charge Amount $ _____

Signature _____

Billing Address _____

Telephone # Day _____ Eve _____

PLEASE NOTE: Your contribution is tax-deductible to the fullest extent allowed by law.
Habitat for Humanity • P.O. Box 1443 • Newport News, VA 23601 • 757-596-5553
www.HelpHabitatforHumanity.org